Postcritical Curriculum in Latin America

This book, drawing on a range of postcritical theories including postmodernism, poststructuralism, and postcolonialism, provides a comprehensive analysis of the current state of curriculum in Latin America.

The book underscores the relationship between curriculum, didactics, and Bildung in the Latino field, acknowledging the hegemony of the United States. It initiates dialogues between scholars from various Latin American countries, promoting the concept of translation and the didactic tradition as a political practice. This practice enables the identification of new scopes and a privileged language, challenging the dominant paradigms and offering fresh perspectives. Recognizing the need for intervention, the book depicts the intellectual history of the field in Argentina and across Latin America. It serves as a critical resource for understanding the complexities and nuances of curriculum studies in the region.

This work will appeal to curriculum studies scholars, researchers, faculty, and postgraduate students worldwide. It offers a unique lens to view and understand the educational landscape in Latin America, making it an indispensable addition to the discourse on curriculum studies and educational research. It challenges readers to rethink traditional approaches and explore new avenues in curriculum studies.

Silvia Morelli is Professor and Research Chair in Curriculum Studies at the National University of Rosario, Argentina.

Studies in Curriculum Theory Series
Series Editor: William F. Pinar, University of British Columbia, Canada

In this age of multimedia information overload, scholars and students may not be able to keep up with the proliferation of different topical, trendy book series in the field of curriculum theory. It will be a relief to know that one publisher offers a balanced, solid, forward-looking series devoted to significant and enduring scholarship, as opposed to a narrow range of topics or a single approach or point of view. This series is conceived as the series busy scholars and students can trust and depend on to deliver important scholarship in the various "discourses" that comprise the increasingly complex field of curriculum theory.

The range of the series is both broad (all of curriculum theory) and limited (only important, lasting scholarship) – including but not confined to historical, philosophical, critical, multicultural, feminist, comparative, international, aesthetic, and spiritual topics and approaches. Books in this series are intended for scholars and for students at the doctoral and, in some cases, master's levels.

Currere from Apartheid to Inclusion
Building Culturally Responsive Pedagogies in Post-Apartheid South Africa
Shani Steyn

Curriculum Fragments
A Currere Journey through Life Processes
Thomas S. Poetter

Curriculum as Confession
The Promise of Teaching for Selfhood and Truth
Christopher M. Cruz

For more information about this series, please visit: https://www.routledge.com/Studies-in-Curriculum-Theory-Series/book-series/LEASCTS

Postcritical Curriculum in Latin America

Policies, Bildung, and US Hegemony

Silvia Morelli

NEW YORK AND LONDON

First published 2025
by Routledge
605 Third Avenue, New York, NY 10158

and by Routledge
4 Park Square, Milton Park, Abingdon, Oxon, OX14 4RN

Routledge is an imprint of the Taylor & Francis Group, an informa business

ISBN: 9781032757025 (hbk)
ISBN: 9781032757032 (pbk)
ISBN: 9781003475279 (ebk)

DOI: 10.4324/9781003475279

Typeset in Times New Roman
by codeMantra

To Ernesto Laclau
(1935–2014)
In memoriam

Contents

Foreword

William F. Pinar

"There are still texts to be written," Silvia Morelli writes, concluding her breakthrough study of *Postcritical Curriculum in Latin America: Policies, Bildung, and US Hegemony*. There remain, she emphasizes, "stories to be redeemed, colleagues to be met in the young and resilient field of the Latin American curriculum." Redemption and resilience are definitely dynamics of this important book that represents another founding moment in the Latin American field.[1] Not only Argentina but also Brazil and Mexico are among those American nations whose curriculum studies scholarships are represented here, but her engagement is not confined to these admittedly key countries in curriculum studies worldwide. "What about curriculum studies in the Caribbean, Cuba and Panama," Morelli asks a crucial question calling scholars there to contribute to the ongoing formation of an authentic – even decolonized – Latin American field. What about Bolivia, Colombia, and Uruguay, she also asks, adding: "What about Afro-American and Indigenous peoples?" From the national Morelli moves to the biocultural, asking: "how is gender represented in Latin American curriculum studies." These – and other – "questions can go on in an attempt to demarcate an ambiguous and complex object, riddled with minimal experiences and hidden histories that have not yet been written." For Morelli as for me: specificity spells solidarity: "every time a Latin American tells an intellectual history or a present circumstance about the curriculum … he or she will be doing so for the field of curriculum in (Latin) America."

As I welcome Silvia Morelli to the select set of scholars who have contributed to Routledge's Series in Curriculum Theory, I want as well to express my gratitude to her for composing the book in English. (I trust it will also appear in Spanish, Portuguese, and French so that readers across the Americas can read what Morelli has achieved.) It is imperative that North American scholars keep abreast with developments in Central and South America, in Latin America overall. And "abreast" we learn this book is, as Morelli approaches Latin American curriculum studies "from post-critical theories, especially post-structuralism and post-modernism." But not only - Morelli will also "enhance the concept of Bildung and analyze the field of curriculum in Latin America in its hegemonic relationship with the United States,"[2] her "poststructuralism from Derrida's translation theory, from Laclau's discourse analysis, and Mouffe's political theory." She focuses on "the formation of a subject whose distinction and difference come from non-hegemonic logics, silenced by modern discourse," a subject whose intellectual identity needs to be defined from a perspective unrelated to the Enlightenment, one that involves their identity and sense of meaning as a Latin American." Morelli states that it is "the conceptual ambiguity of Bildung, [that] allows [me] to recover the so-called *Bildung-centred Didaktik* for the field of school instruction and in it its relationship with the curriculum."[3]

Morelli writes to us from Argentina, "the country where my grandparents arrived trying to leave the European chaos between the wars, carrying in their trunks objects that accompanied me all my childhood and that I later found in the one-way trips that the curriculum granted me." It was Argentina, she reminds, "that in 1884 sanctioned its first public, free and secular Education Act, which managed to educate not only the children of immigrants who attended school, but also their foreign parents." A country that was once the beacon of Latin America, offering its inhabitants access to culture, education, health and social mobility. However, the wear and tear of dictatorships and the last 40 years of democracy have altered its former achievements. "It is the curriculum studies," Morelli confides, "that allowed me to transform the pain and worry that this causes me."

Not curriculum studies *tout court*, but a constellation her own situatedness enables her to see, constellation an idea Morelli extracts from a 2016 Museum of Modern Art exhibition, *A Japanese Constellation: Toyo Ito, SANAA, and Beyond*, curated by Pedro Gadanho,[4] the concept of constellation decoded as a network of luminaries at work, emphasizing "network" as a "sensibility" that is passed through individual artists or, in this case, Latin American curriculum studies, theorists. Morelli writes:

I am interested in recovering the constellation as a metaphor to identify the configuration of curriculum studies in Latin America. These are consolidated through events that foster intellectual conversations and creations that account for the growth of this field. Likewise, I recognize those who train others in topics specific to our region and influence those already trained or those at the beginning of their careers. To this end, I approach the constellations considering two key instances: one of them is the influence exerted by some academics, who stand out in the plot, and the other is training as a pedagogical process of knowledge transmission.

Structured, then, by categories such as "influence" and "training," the constellations Morelli identifies – especially in Mexico and Brazil – are those that "develop post-critical curriculum studies and, in my opinion, are two groups that articulate training in the rest of the Latin continent."

"The constellations are integrated by academic generations," Morelli continues, "by collaborations between other generations from other countries" as well as "by non-Latin influences and formations and by the institutions in which the groups are nucleated." These constellations have been "built with both foreign and local influences," and there are also "links between them." Morelli emphasizes "in these two groups the passage from critical Marxist theory to post-Marxist and post-structuralist theories in the construction of categories of analysis for curriculum theory." In Brazil, for example, she identifies two theorists who have been especially influential, Antonio Flavio Moreira of the Federal University of Rio de Janeiro, and Tomaz Tadeu da Silva of the Federal University of Rio Grande do Sul, both of whom carved a "passage from critical curriculum theory to postmodern perspectives." Having studied at the University of London and influenced by Michael Young, enabling him to bring "critical English curricular notions to the Brazilian context," Moreira "made contributions to the theory and history of curriculum and multiculturalism, establishing the relationship between curriculum, culture and difference." He has had "a direct influence on [Alice] Casimiro Lopes and [Elizabeth] Macedo," both on the faculty of the State University of Rio de Janeiro. Tomaz Tadeu da Silva also moved from Marxism, but unlike Moreira, da Silva emphasized "the subject and identity as the two problems of modernity, although he poses them as small narratives, resisting the large narratives." The "passage to postmodern and poststructuralist perspectives is complemented by what was initiated by Moreira and Silva, although it should be noted that it is consolidated with the discourse theory of Laclau and Mouffe," evident in the "use of the categories of discourse, articulation and difference, as well as in political categories such as hegemony, democracy and conflict." This "Laclau-Mouffe binomial is enhanced when the Brazilian constellation enters poststructuralism by taking Derrida's translation and deconstruction as a language to understand the curriculum politically," characterizing curriculum policies "as a discursive and undecidable construction, lacking fixed rules and unpredictable."

"The density of the Mexican constellation," Morelli reports, "has been growing steadily since the early 1970s." She cites Raquel Glazman and María de Ibarrola who "made the curriculum visible through *Design of Study Plan*," then Ángel Díaz Barriga, Alicia de Alba, Concepción Barrón Tirado, Frida Díaz Barriga Arceo and José María García Garduño, scholars whose interventions "materialize the constellations," the Brazilian constellation with "delimited borders and is profound, while the Mexican constellation has permeable borders (inside and outside the country) and comprises a wider range of topics." The two constellations "maintain a dialogue," characterized "by common theories and shared categories, but also by assumed differences." In December 2023, this dialogue – extended to Argentina and Chile – resulted in the establishment of the Latin American Network of Curriculum Studies.

Morelli identifies four concepts characterizing the field today: "hybridism, culture, difference and technological change." Hybridism, Morelli reports, "is recovered by José María García Garduño, associating the concept with *mestizaje*, and so it's also "an anthropological category," of which "Latin America is a living example." "A hybrid construction can be uncomfortable and uncommon" – García Garduño offers *Spanglish* as instance of hybridization of speech developed by Latinos in the United States and Canada – and Morelli adds "*Portuñol*, which is the mixture of Portuguese and Spanish languages (originated in the triple border between Argentina, Brazil, and Uruguay)." Casimiro Lopes "refers to hybridity as the loss of a common language and the accumulation of knowledge," even "considering it through the metaphor of libraries," also as a "category to rethink the stability with which history is constructed." Morelli thinks of hybridity in "epistemological terms," evident in Brazilian curriculum studies in "the relationship between disciplinarity and transdisciplinarity in the study of subjects." Morelli invokes Hongyu Wang's emphasis upon the "third space" or the space of the "in-between," for Wang also "an autobiographical journey in which the subject has to deal with himself and with otherness." And there is García Canclini's sense of hybridity as a "bridge that cushions the passage from the modern to the postmodern, that can be identified as a cultural reconciliation." Hybridity, Morelli concludes, "allows Latin American post-pandemic curricula to build other perspectives from which to approach the school class, micropolitical decisions, the identity of subjects and all that, unforeseen, that relates to new cultural systems, deterritorialization and impure genres."

"New cultural systems" and "impure genres" intermingle in the concept of "mestizos," in the omnipresence of which "racism is disguised" and "native peoples and Afro-Americans" underemphasized. Morelli is here citing Gallardo Gutiérrez, who points out that "the flow of migrations, throughout the history of America, creates new interculturalities that deserve to be considered in the curricula." Also in play is Alicia de Alba's notion of "cultural contact," which "makes it possible to recognize, know and value diversity," but which can create intercultural relationships characterized by "inequality, conflict and the production of new identities," resulting in defensive "self-segregation" and "marginalization of native Mexican cultures."

The concept of "difference" constitutes "one of the categories around which the Brazilian constellation is organized," Morelli notes, a concept that "not only institutes particular identity, but also assumes the non-predictability of events, the argument that all difference is political and the lack of a center of domination." There is concern "that 'difference' is being suffocated by the specter of equality and diverse identities." Morelli cites Macedo's suggestion that "equality and difference have their own political dynamics that cannot be analyzed in a generic way," that "contingency is always involved."

"Technological change" is another key concept in Latin American curriculum studies. Schools' preoccupations with technological change – here Morelli is citing de Alba – can mean the "exclusion" of other subjects. Certainly, that's the case in the United States, where technologies companies have lobbied to replace, in the secondary school curriculum, the study of foreign language with coding.[5] "New social spaces, with different materialities, [are] created by technological change," encouraging life "online." In 2019, U.S. teenagers spent over seven hours each day online,[6] a number likely to have increased in the five years since – and not only in the United States.

"It is already known that no text is spared from being translated," Morelli reminds, and when translation takes place, it's "never linear, not even from one document to another." Region matters, including in Argentina, where "24 different translations" take place, translations "that correspond to the jurisdictions in which the curriculum is organized (23 provinces and the autonomous city of Buenos Aires)." When "perceiving translation as a micropolitical practice, the teacher becomes the translator and the author of the curriculum." The death-of-the-author[7] be damned, I, too, proclaim.[8] The same fate for the death-of-the-subject[9] and "when Argentina and Brazil choose concepts such as 'school trajectories' and 'life project' they awaken the reader's imagination towards biographical, subjective, self-reflective processes that make visible the student and his or her formation process within the school." Within neoliberal curriculum policy, it is a specific formation politicians prefer, namely the "entrepreneur," a subject position presumably achievable through school "success," individual achievement, "far from proposing collective activities," and leaving nothing to chance, "no room for contingency, always seeking indispensable conditions of necessity and the idea of a foreseeable future."

"Without as much centrality as the 'life project' of Brazil's curriculum or the 'school trajectories' of Argentina's," Morelli explains, "Mexico's design mentions a 'personal project' as the interaction between each student's learning and the content offered by the teacher." So how "personal" can such a "project" be? Like so-called helicopter parents, politicians want teachers to monitor minutia, accomplish what parents can't, namely the formation of the child in "spiritual, ethical, moral, affective, intellectual, artistic and physical dimensions, through the transmission and cultivation of values, knowledge and skills," a dazzling array Morelli quotes from Chile's "Curricular Bases for Secondary Education" of 2015. While upholding "freedom of education and the right to education as core concepts," Chile's policy – "almost in line with Brazil's design" – "encourages students to elaborate 'the first definitions' of a life project that allows them to assume commitments and responsibilities." Freedom through commitment and responsibility? Orwellian doublethink.[10]

"As a politically impossible task," Morelli points out, "Latin American curricular policies focus on 'the common' pretending to achieve inclusion of all diversities (cultural, social, racial, gender, etc.)," but "decided in the heat of hegemony, this concept only encourages exclusion." Morelli knows:

"Nothing is more impersonal than the common to all, nothing more misguided than the illusion of believing in the common as a condition for everyone to be represented in the curriculum," and "this," she suggests, "is the most important problem afflicting Latin American curriculum policies," as "creating a condition of the common that does no more than confirm that there is knowledge more valuable than other and that the denomination of common presents a partiality granted by power relations." So, the "great challenge for Latin American curricula" is "includ[ing] everyone without homogenizing the subjects that are included." In any case, recall that "it is in the translation made by teachers as authors of the curriculum in each school, where this discourse acquires materiality and meaning."

And speaking of meaning, Morelli returns to *Bildung*, wondering if it "makes sense in Latin America," for her "a propitious question that enables me to study its meaning and its relationship with society and school in the unstable and convulsed present times," adding: "I admit the fascination that the concept of *Bildung* provokes in me when I think of formation associated with the relationship between curriculum and *Didakitk*," as the two "can be understood as a single field." She reminds that "post-critical theories distrust the idea of the subject because of the centrality it has taken in modernity," noting that "revising it implies inscribing it in the relationship with the environment, multiculturalism, language, accepting that each case will be a small, minimal and particular narrative." Such postmodern "subjects emerge from silences and invisibility, manifesting themselves through feminisms, disabilities, sexual identities, blackness and anything that highlights difference." And so "a challenge presented by an idea of post-*Bildung* is to rethink the subject in the tension between itself and theories such as that proposed by post-humanism, which includes not only human beings, but extends its consideration to other living beings," moving Morelli to position "the subject in an intermediate space between humanism, questioning the arrogance with which man has occupied the center of history, and post-humanism."

In "rescuing the ambiguity of the concept of *Bildung*," Morelli reasons, "it is not only the relationship of the subject with society that deserves to be analyzed, but, above all, the relationship of the subjects with themselves, with their inwardness and with what they wish to be." So, she returns to "the nodal questions of the formation process, contained in *Bildung* and continued in post-*Bildung*: Who am I and what do I want to become, who am I as a (Latin)American and what do I want to become in order to continue being (Latin)American?" To the primacy of the political in many efforts to contextualize curriculum Morelli adds "another more personal, interior, subjective question with which the subject continues to grapple with itself in the thick journey of their formation." Nowadays, however, "the construction of the *self* is installed in times in which the principle of reality has been abandoned, … times of selfies with which the subject presents himself in society, changing their own image, fabricating another one that deceives the viewer of the image. This distortion is part of the subject that pretends to be self-determined in the eyes of others." Rather than profilicity[11] – self-determination in the eyes of others – Morelli invokes Klafki's "three moments of *Bildung*," in its relation to his "critical-constructive didactics" … composed of self-determination, co-determination and solidarity." In the constellation created by their interrelatedness incubates what Fanon – a man of Martinique – wanted half-a-century ago: "[F]or humanity, comrades, … we must work out new concepts, and try to set afoot a new man."[1]

"New concepts" are born from old ones. Morelli narrates the history of curriculum studies in Latin America, the "first event" being "the translation into Spanish and distribution of works inscribed in the *Curriculum Development* movement," this event was orchestrated by the *Alliance for Progress* between 1961 and 1970. The "second event" was the "standardization of curricular discourses," that enforced by the World Bank and the Inter-American Development Bank during the 1990s. Such "reforms construct a notion of curriculum as a technological device that directs educational improvement towards social and economic growth," and, "as a neo-technicist event," it "reissues evaluation as educational accreditation and elaborates a taxonomy of contents that organize educational competencies." Invoking Badiou, Morelli decodes "event" as both "rupture and possibility," and so she sees "the possibility of constructing the history and epistemology of the Latin American curriculum with another approach, with other subjects, recognizing other circumstances," recognizing, "as if it were an interactive puzzle, [that] all of America is assembled by colonizations, migrations, violence of all kinds that silence voices, erase cultures, neutralize languages, discriminate races, annihilate lives," requiring curriculum scholars "to place ourselves in the rupture as an intermediate space to question the hegemony with which the history of the curriculum is recognized, with its technical, rational and efficient perspective that guarantees social control and annuls the differences of practices." From such questioning ruptures appear in the scarred surface of the palimpsest that is the present of the Americas: North, Central, South – one America Morelli reminds.

"All of America is a conquered continent that bears in its name the mark of that conquest," Morelli knows. "Our languages are imposed, as a result of the negation of other languages, the objects of cultural subjugation." While feeling "familiar" and indeed "like our own," these "ways of naming … are alien." An "impossible act," Morelli suggests that "translation" positions "the reader at the crossroads of having to choose between oblivion and negation." Only "the naive reader denies the translation and ignores the linguistic filter of the culture that plays all the time with signifiers and meanings." No naïve

1 Fanon 1968, 316.

reader, Morelli knows that the "ambiguity of Latin America in curriculum studies" derives from the fact that the field "oscillates between the tradition of U.S. technicism, with which it enters the world of curriculum, and the critical sociological proposals that understand education as a political act and the curriculum as its point of resistance." It is the continent's history of "dictatorships, revolutions, oppression, repression, exclusion, injustice, [and] inequality [that] allowed critical theory to flourish as a safeguard for curriculum studies." Here she cites "Paulo Freire's emancipatory educational ideas" that "have inscribed social praxis in the curriculum, turning it into a construction that acquires the forms and categories of politics." "This is," Morelli concludes, the "identity" of Latin America: "Resistance is the defense mechanism that allows the continent to maintain its identity."

"Latin America is always," it seems to Morelli, "in an intermediate space between revolution and progress, belonging and exclusion, subjugation and negation," and in "these interstices are the germs of the identity of the Latin American curriculum studies." A "territory born of hegemony in 1492," Latin America "oscillates between the Modernity that gave it structure and the postmodernity that warns it of the cracking of the idea of people, school and common curriculum; between the critical theory that provides it with categories for liberation and the post-critical theories that highlight minorities and their differences, allowing everything to be possible; between the globalization to which it was obligatorily invited to participate and the internationalization that allows it to hold complicated conversations with others that are just as different." Insofar as it imposes standardization, globalization could be considered a form of neocolonialism. For Morelli, "the inquisitorial sentence of the multilateral credit organizations on Latin American education confirms the subjugation controlled by the standardization that does not fit the measures of the continent. Nothing could be more inappropriate than reports and recommendations on the state of education based on foreign criteria and unattainable objectives."

In contrast – insofar as internationalization denotes dialogical encounters across differences, it denotes decolonization, as an ideal unattainable but as a pedagogical practice obligatory. In curriculum studies – as in other fields grappling with its conceptual occupation by concepts estranged from the specificity of the local – that means attending to intellectual history of the field. For Latin American curriculum studies, Morelli writes, "the first task is to define the relations with the United States and European countries as providers of theories and perspectives of analysis that have affected the field," admittedly a "difficult task of questioning the theories with which we have been formed," but one "that uproots colonialism," those "naturalized relations of subalternity that condition curriculum theory and school practices." So, "the construction of Post-*Bildung* for the process of formation of a post-pandemic Latin American subject calls for solidarity as the third moment of the *Didaktik* centered on *Bildung*," but "also to attend to the metaphorical fiction of literature and its characters, who carry the problems of femininities, négritudes and disabilities, narrated in first person, in Latin American territories." Such solidarity supports "characters who resist the circumstances of their formation processes, characters that reflect on their identity and what they want to become." Such a concept of "Post-*Bildung* will make sense if it takes up again the debate of the subject configured by multiple literacies in which the force of the moving image is greater than that of writing," ours an ocularcentric age wherein the "screen" becomes a "*black mirror* returns the density of a distorted identity, filtered, modified by the aesthetics of consumption." Now "it is more profitable to show happiness than intelligence, it is more profitable the capacity of consumption than the formation of the subject."

"Without wishing to be apocalyptic," Morelli winks, "or to suggest that the concept of (Post) *Bildung* will be the salvation of the subject through its formation, I consider it pertinent to attend to the pedagogical core, of relationship with others and of reflection with oneself that it proposes in order to rethink the subject of postmodernity." However, besieged by technology, consumer capitalism, cultural fragmentation and political polarization, "relationship" is surely "the pedagogical core." That insight is embedded in Morelli's reactivation of *Bildung*; she knows that the celebrated (and critiqued) concept "has the articulatory capacity to find a place between curriculum theory and the *Didaktik* tradition (*Didaktik Tradiciton*)." Solidarity through specificity can support the challenge, that is, "to face the decisions of the silenced Latin American voices so that the process of formation makes the subject visible and vice versa." Morelli has indeed made the "subject visible."

In making her subject – Latin American curriculum studies – visible, Morelli has translated a dynamic centrifugal field into a constellation at which we readers can gaze, knowing that its light has taken time to reach us. Not the hundreds of thousands of years distant stars' light can take, but time nonetheless, and so we know that the constellation we see here – lighting up our sky – contains concepts we cannot yet see. Silvia points the way, not only in her stunning sense of "constellation" – what a brilliant choice of metaphors for the field – but also in Morelli's mapping of its specific intellectual histories and present circumstances, histories marked by movements from Marxism to poststructuralism, structured by European concepts made almost native by Latin American theorists and scholars, no endpoint, of course, but instead a series of (inter)stellar conceptual events rupturing the present as they point to future possibilities, including, perhaps, a Latin theory of *Post-Bildung*. These are among the many promising possibilities of this "young and resilient field" – as Morelli so perfectly puts it – the light of which burns bright, the field of Latin American curriculum studies that curriculum scholars worldwide will want to watch. Our collective thanks go to Silvia Morelli for serving as our astronomer.

Notes

1 Surely the first was Mardones (2018).
2 *Bildung* is a term I juxtapose – even blend with – *currere*: Pinar (2011a). Mexican scholars too attend to their field's invasion from the United States, specifically the enforcement of the so-called Tyler Rationale: Pinar (2011b).
3 In her study of nineteenth British culture, Amanda Anderson (2001, p. 4) emphasizes *Bildung* as "the self-reflexive cultivation of character, which animated much of Victorian ethics and aesthetics, from John Stuart Mill to Matthew Arnold and beyond." As Morelli's project emphasizes, *Bildung* is a concept that was – is – hardly confined to Germany – or to Europe.
4 https://www.gsd.harvard.edu/person/pedro-gadanho/.
5 https://www.highereddive.com/news/should-coding-replace-foreign-language-requirements/590435/.
6 https://abcnews.go.com/US/teens-spend-hours-screens-entertainment-day-report/story?id=66607555#:~:text=Teens%20spend%20an%20average%20of%20seven%20hours%20and,that%20promotes%20safe%20technology%20and%20media%20for%20children.
7 Associated with Barthes of course: https://literariness.org/2016/03/20/roland-barthes-concept-of-death-of-the-author/.
8 Pinar (2023, pp. 87–105).
9 https://www.marxists.org/reference/subject/philosophy/works/en/heartfield-james.htm.
10 https://www.theatlantic.com/magazine/archive/2019/07/1984-george-orwell/590638/.
11 Pinar (2023, p. 212ff).

References

Anderson, A. (2001). *The Powers of Distance. Cosmopolitanism and the Cultivation of Detachment*. Princeton University Press.

Fanon, F. (1968). *The Wretched of the Earth*. [Preface by Jean-Paul Sartre. Trans. by Constance Farrington.] Grove Press.

Mardones, D. F. J. (2018). *Curriculum Studies as an International Conversation: Educational Traditions and Cosmopolitanism in Latin America*. Routledge.

Pinar, W. F. (2011a). *The Character of Curriculum Studies: Bildung, Currere, and the Recurring Question of the Subject*. Palgrave Macmillan.

Pinar, W. F. (Ed.). (2011b). *Curriculum Studies in Mexico: Intellectual Histories, Present Circumstances*. Palgrave Macmillan.

Pinar, W. F. (2023). *A Praxis of Presence*. Routledge.

Acknowledgments

I want to express my gratitude to William F. Pinar for the invitation to publish this book. From the moment we met in 2013, Bill has done nothing more than encourage my formation, demonstrating his unconditional trust in me.

To Alicia de Alba, for having transported me toward post-critical theories, and her offer, as a path of no return, to enter in CXXI.

To Alice Casimiro Lopes, Daniel Johnson Mardones, Ana Gallardo Gutiérrez, and Camila Carlachiani who provided access to documentation on the curriculum policies of each country. Likewise, I am very grateful for the time that I needed to consult them, and they offered their willingness to debate.

All my gratitude to Cecilia Berchansky who made possible the translation of this text, first written in Spanish, into English taking care of every detail.

To the groups that make up the Latin community in curriculum studies and where I find friendship, solidarity, and academia: GCA, *Seminario Curriculum Latinoamericano* (Latin American Curriculum Seminar), NECCEE, and the recently created *Red Latinoamericana de Estudios Curriculares/Rede Latino-Americana de Estudos Curriculares*. Everything I learned with them is reflected in these pages.

Thank you all for the love, passion, and trust.

Acronyms and Abbreviations

AAACS	American Association for the Advancement of Curriculum Studies
ACSA	Australian Curriculum Studies Association
BCU	British Columbia University
BNCC	Common National Curriculum Base
CCE	Emerging Curriculum Code
CEG	Generalized Structural Crisis
CEICyD	Center for Studies and Research on Curriculum and Didactics
CFE	Federal Council of Education
CLACSO	Latin American Council of Social Sciences
COMIE	Mexican Council for Educative Investigation
CXXI	Curriculum and the 21st Century
EIB	Intercultural Bilingual Education
Euro-ACS	European Association of Curriculum Studies
GCA	Argentina Curriculum Group
HNU	Hangzhou Normal University
IAACS	International Association for the Advancement of Curriculum Studies
ICE	Curriculum and Evaluation Institute
IISUE	University and Education Research Institute
LSU	Louisiana State University
LTG	Free textbooks
MoMA	Museum of Modern Art
NECCEE	Core Study Curriculum, Knowledge, and School Experience
PROPED	Graduate Program in Education
SEP	Secretary of Public Education
UACM	Autonomous University of Mexico City
UASLP	Autonomous University of San Luis Potosí
UAZ	Autonomous University of Zacatecas
UBA	University of Buenos Aires
UChile	University of Chile
UERJ	State University of Rio de Janeiro

UFRGS	Federal University of Río Grande do Sul
UFRJ	Federal University of Rio de Janeiro
UNAM	National Autonomous University of Mexico
UNIPE	National Pedagogical University
UNLZ	National University of Lomas de Zamora
UNPSJB	Patagonia National University San Juan Bosco
UNR	National University of Rosario
UOTTAWA	University of Ottawa

1 Introduction

How do I get here

In September 1990, when I was a few months away from finishing my undergraduate degree, I found an opening to be a Student Assistant in the subject "Área del Curriculum" (Curriculum Area). It was not in my plans to be trained in Curriculum Studies, but I do not know what led me to apply, register, and get the position. An inner and instinctive calling had intervened, leading me on a one-way road, from which I would never return. Complicated years would come for me in Argentina. An economic crisis that made it difficult for me to survive as a university teacher combined with the incipient postgraduate careers that were emerging in a country that ten years earlier had been under a dictatorship. The beginning of a global era in which reforms rode to the rhythm of neoliberalism marked the perimeter in which the decade would pass. This hostile, uncomfortable scenario, plagued with limitations, was compensated by my training in the curriculum. First came the translations of curriculum theory that the Spanish academics made from the Anglo-Saxon field. These were tempered by my interest in the Social Theory and Critical Philosophy of the Frankfurt School. I pursued the books published in Spanish by Max Horkheimer, Theodor Adorno, and Jürgen Habermas, and I made them interact with those of Martin Jay, Thomas McCarthy, and Susan Buck-Morss. I was trying to give a greater philosophical foundation to a field that was discredited in Argentina, such as that of the curriculum, which, responding to an epistemological tradition that was little explained, was inclined to consider Didactics as the great epistemic territory in which the curriculum was a thematic appendix.

It would be unfair of me if I did not acknowledge that in Argentina during the 1990s many works on curriculum were published, mostly theoretical approaches or practical demarcations that allowed us to understand what a reform was about or how to manage a curriculum at school. Even those academics who later denied the existence of curriculum as an intellectual field were encouraged to talk about it in the painful decade of curriculum reforms. When I was Teacher Assistant, in the merciless days of university life, where any academic becomes an enemy to pick up the crumbs that fell on the floor, a toxic colleague asked me why I was studying curriculum, if everything

DOI: 10.4324/9781003475279-1

was already written in this field. I confess that I was never so disturbed by mediocrity as I was at that time. So much so that since then I remember it as if it were still happening. I have also commented on it in different classes, with those who circumstantially occupied the place of students. But I also remember the feeling of annoyance and desperation that I experienced when I wanted to respond by refuting a thesis for which the answer was unknown to me. Very sure to confirm that the field of curriculum was not exhausted; I was unaware of where it was going. Up to that point, what had been written on curriculum consolidating the field in the region was disseminated by Michael Apple, Ángel Díaz Barriga, Alicia de Alba, and Henry Giroux. The book *Curriculum: Product or Praxis* by Shirley Grundy was recited as a Marxist manifesto on Curriculum Theory in "Área del Curriculum" (Curriculum Area) of the National University of Rosario (UNR). It was easy to confirm that it was all written. And it was a very comfortable position to convince oneself that there was no need to continue writing. But a suspicion awakened the dissatisfaction that led me to believe that there was much more and that despite the state of this field in Argentina, other academics were producing contributions not known to me until then. Looking for answers, chance, and fortune took me out of that uncomfortable zone and the first event in my biography occurred.

In 2006, Alicia de Alba gave a seminar at the Patagonia National University San Juan Bosco (UNPSJB), in the city of Comodoro Rivadavia. I flew there, looking for pending answers on the continuity of the field. I found an author who was changing her critical stance toward a postmodern and anti-essentialist one, after having studied with Ernesto Laclau during her stay at the University of Essex. The seminar consisted of what the following year would become her book *Curriculum-sociedad El peso de la incertidumbre, la fuerza de la imaginación* (Curriculum-society. The weight of uncertainty, the power of imagination). Once her book was published, I invited Alicia to give the seminar at the UNR in order to spread the information among my colleagues from Rosario regarding what was being produced on curriculum. By then, my training was not only advancing in curriculum studies through Alicia de Alba, but also in discourse analysis. At that time, I was studying to obtain a Master's Degree in Communication Sciences, searching in social communication for arguments to think of the curriculum as a text. In the study of discourse as social production of meaning, I recognized Ernesto Laclau from a political perspective and Eliseo Verón from a semiotic perspective. Their theories allowed me to finish my thesis entitled *Discursos curriculares: entre la política de los 90 y el imaginario social* (Curriculum discourses: between the politics of the 90s and the social imaginary) in 2009. A heartbreaking moment was when, within two days of each other, Ernesto Laclau first and Eliseo Verón later passed away in 2014. The void caused by both absences anticipated that two theories would cease to be written, at least by their authors. At the same time, orphaned of theoretical mentors, I inherited the invitation to become the author of my own texts.

Alicia de Alba's seminar at UNPSJB allowed me to be part, from 2007 to 2015, of the "Seminario Curriculum y Siglo XXI" (CXXI) (Seminar Curriculum and the 21st century), coordinated by Bertha Orozco at the *Instituto de Investigaciones sobre la Universidad y la Educación* (IISUE) at the National Autonomous University of Mexico (UNAM), which was developed with annual in-person meetings (which I used to attend) and via Skype. The deepening of discourse theory, poststructuralist readings of Foucault for the field of curriculum, and studies of curricular reforms carried out in Latin America were the constant topics discussed at the CXXI. Guided by Jean-François Lyotard's *The Postmodern Condition*, I have opted for a theory of curriculum that questions the legitimacy of truth as a condition for understanding the scientific. I am opposed to sustaining the most important narratives because I consider that their universality is insufficient to understand the social complexities of today. The study of the curriculum in discourse perspective, initiated with Laclau and Veron, led me to Political Philosophy, field in which authors such as Jacques Rancière and Chantal Mouffe are prominent. At the same time, I recover the poststructuralist Foucault that has left me on the threshold of Derrida's writings, a philosopher that I continue to discover in my dialogue with colleagues at the State University of Rio de Janeiro. This is the best argument I find to explain to myself the interest in curricular policies as constructions that do not respect verticality, nor condition themselves among their levels.

A turning point becomes the second event. At the end of 2012, the UNR approves my doctoral thesis project entitled *Horizontes teóricos para la construcción conceptual del campo del curriculum. Lecturas desde América Latina* (Theoretical horizons for the conceptual construction of the curriculum field. Readings from Latin America). While, in January 2013, it is presented at the University and Education Research Institute (IISUE) *Curriculum Studies in Mexico. Intellectual Histories, Present Circumstances*, edited by William Pinar. Alice Casimiro Lopes from UERJ and William Pinar from the University of British Columbia (UBC) participated as guest lecturers. To persuade myself that organizing a trip in a few days was the right thing to do, I said to myself: "what am I doing in Rosario, if the curriculum is being discussed in Mexico City." From that moment, driven by the writing of my doctoral thesis on the curriculum in Argentina and Mexico and accompanied by intellectuals like Bill and Alice, another chapter starts in my Argentine history related to this field that I had once been provocatively told was "all written."

William Pinar's generous passion for curriculum studies, where he intervenes, allows for the growth of both this intellectual field and the scholars within it. Having read some of his books allowed me not only to articulate stories, characters, and circumstances, but also to learn academic writing in English. As I have said ever since, moved by the enjoyment of reading Pinar, I learned to write in English. Reading Pinar, too, I met Bill Doll (Jr.) by letting him convey to me his admiration for him. Discovered in one of his texts I exclaimed to myself, who is this man! With Pinar as a born articulator of curriculum studies, internationalization is presented as a task that offers resistance to globalization, opposing it. I believe that, after the moment of reconceptualization, Pinar managed to install in the new century, the moment of internationalization of curriculum studies by leading the academics of the world to feel the need to express their opinion on the particularity and history of curriculum in their countries. His two collections, one of them being both *Handbooks of Curriculum Research* and the other the collection called *Curriculum Studies. Intellectual Histories, Present Circumstances* (for the cases of Brazil, and Mexico), allowed me to learn about the state of the field in the Spanish speaking countries. I was discovering who "represent" each country and from what perspective they understood the curriculum, I was understanding their curriculum's histories. In the case of my Argentine colleagues Mariano Palamidessi, Daniel Feldman, Silvina Feeney, and Flavia Terigi, they wrote about the curriculum in a country that prioritized didactics. However, internationalization also materialized in events organized by the International Association for the Advancement of Curriculum Studies (IAACS), created for that purpose, the American Association for the Advancement of Curriculum Studies, and the European Association for Curriculum Studies (Euro-ACS). Participating in their events was not only the possibility to socialize what I was studying, but also what we were discussing in the CXXI or other Latin American teams. New faces, at least for me, such as Eero Ropo, Tero Autio, Janet Miller, Elizabeth Macedo, Michael Uljens, Daniel Johnson, and Molly Queen, did nothing more than to institute the beginning of new meetings. In Latin America, it was Mexico and Brazil, and then Chile that continued this tradition. I would like to thank the IISUE of UNAM, the *Programa de Pós Graduação em Educação* (Pro-PEd) of UERJ, and the Core Study Curriculum, Knowledge, and School Experience (NECCEE) of the Faculty of Social Sciences of the University of Chile (UChile) for having hosted me as a guest so many times, allowing me to learn through solidarity and empathy.

I have the best memories of the fifth Triennial International Association for the Advancement of Curriculum Studies Conference at the University of Ottawa (UOttawa), in 2015, where the spirit of Ted Aoki was in the air and William Pinar occupied a nodal place. I admiringly enjoyed the presentations entitled *Who is William F. Pinar?* by Maria Luiza Süssekind from the Federal University of Rio de Janeiro (UFRJ); *Study: An Undervalued Concept and Activity?*, presented by Pinar himself, Anne Phelan and Claudia Ruitenberg both from British Columbia University (BCU); and *The 'Power of the Possible' in Seemingly Impossible Times: Celebrating and Honoring the Legacy of Maxine Greene* presented by Janet Miller from Columbia University, William Pinar (BCU), Elizabeth Macedo (UERJ), and Zhang Hua from Hangzhou Normal University (HNU). I would like to highlight the lucidity of the group of scholars from Lousiana State University (LSU) and BCU. My participation in *The School Bus Symposium: A Journey of Sensory Experience*[1] (McLarnon et al., 2016) was the instance that confirmed that I was thinking curriculum in the right place and that led me, while riding the school bus around the city of Ottawa, to the exercise of what Pinar (2011a) calls *currere*. That symposium allowed me to write the following:

> *Along a Yellow School Bus in Ottawa*
>
> Silvia Morelli, Universidad Nacional de Rosario (Argentina)
>
> Beauty, everything is beauty. The sun shines in the yellow school bus. And it is filled with memories from childhood, from my own life, from my own story, warm and quiet. While we are traveling, a deep emotion surrounds my soul. What happens in Ottawa, so far from Rosario? The memories travel through time and space and I am still on my own. I feel like I am six years old in a yellow school bus in Ottawa, so far from my home, but not from my memories.
>
> All is beauty, hope, future, love. All is beautiful, like it was when I was a girl. The school bus moves along the neighborhoods, and I move along myself, along my own history, stitching school memories seals in my soul. School is not uncommon to me, but it surprises me. I am *a foreigner* in Ottawa. I am so far home. A stranger is sharing her feelings to the Yellow School Bus. I remember my sons. I can't avoid bring to present their own stories of the yellow school bus and memories from the adventure in their childhood. Both are brave boys waiting for me in Rosario. And I wonder how many feelings from childhood they have and still don't know, how many memories they have that I don't know.
>
> In the bustle, a wide-eyed girl, I keep the silence of introspection. The yellow school bus that takes me along Ottawa's neighborhoods takes me along my school memories, a long time ago, so far away. Love is a beautiful color. All is sunshine, wood, green, pace, emotion. They are traces of my childhood: a bright yellow school bus in a sunny spring afternoon in Ottawa.
>
> (McLarnon et al., 2016, p. 150)

My gratitude to Nicholas Ng-A-Fook and Awad Ibrahim, Conference Chairs, for the successful organization of the event and their hospitality, making me feel part of the IAACS family. Once back home in Rosario, I wrote an email to Pinar telling him that "I would never have imagined that the curriculum would make me so happy." A phrase that years later Tero Autio used with me in an email.

The desire to make the curriculum field visible in Argentina was an incessant struggle that became more agile when I met Marina, through Bertha Orozco, Marina Paulozzo, from the National University of Lomas de Zamora (UNLZ). Marina is a fierce defender of the curricular field that, had it not been for the activities organized by UNAM, I would not have known. This continued to confirm the weakness of the curriculum field in

Argentina that, in order for two scholars to meet, they had to do so through the consolidation of the Mexican field. By 2015, the Curriculum and Evaluation Institute (ICE) of UNLZ organized academic discussion seminars on various curriculum issues. The team from the Center for Studies and Research on Curriculum and Didactics (CEICyD) of the UNR went there. That month of August, in which the roads that connect Rosario with the city of Buenos Aires, an obligatory passing point to reach Lomas de Zamora, were cut off by floods and overflows of the Paraná River. That academic trip would become an odyssey, six hours to get there and another six hours to return, which could only be sustained by the passion that the passengers had for the curricular studies. UNLZ had also invited academics from the University of Buenos Aires (UBA) to this meeting. All of us who were there shared the need to give more formality and continuity to curriculum studies in Argentina. By the end of the event, a virtual communication with Alicia de Alba confirmed the imperative of maintaining periodic meetings between Argentine universities while keeping in touch with Latin American universities. The meetings to make the curriculum field visible in Argentina had an annual, although random, rhythm. These were complemented by a Latin American meeting on the occasion of the CLACSO Congress in the city of Buenos Aires and the Seminar *Curriculum-sociedad. Voces, tensiones y perspectivas* (Curriculum-Society. Voices, Tensions and Perspectives) organized to commemorate the tenth anniversary of IISUE in Mexico City. However, the organization starts to function with greater formality, among professors of Argentine national universities who belonged to this field with two seminars at National Pedagogical University (UNIPE) in 2018 and 2019. The pandemic years kept the meetings with a more organized frequency that allowed more academic events and the creation of the Argentina Curriculum Group (GCA, Grupo Curriculum Argentina), in 2021. In 2022, we launched with Camila Carlachiani the master's degree in Curriculum Studies at UNR, which allows us to form a group of potential curriculum specialists, to organize the research in this field and to give visibility, at least in Latin America, to the curriculum. What is striking is that within two years, the master's degree achieves what could not be done in the ten years of CEICyD, an honorary study center that was sustained with a lot of fluctuation of members, activities, and publications, some of them unfinished.

The concern of Alice Casimiro Lopes and Alicia de Alba led to the launching in December 2023 of the Latin American Curriculum Studies Network/ Rede Latinoamericana do Estudos Curriculares at the UERJ, which at the time of writing this book already has representatives from most of the countries and more than 150 members. Through this network, we intend to strengthen inter-institutional relations in the continent by promoting studies, publications, meetings, and, above all, the continuity and growth of the curriculum in the region.

About this book

This book deals with the curriculum in Latin America with the challenge of approaching it from postcritical theories, especially poststructuralism, and postmodernism. Responding to those who argue that in the field of curriculum, everything has been written and after my training with colleagues from Mexico and Brazil, I have been working with these theories for almost two decades. I do not rule out the possibility of further advances in curriculum theory from Hermeneutics and Critical Sciences. In my opinion, the current social problems that require curricular approaches take on an accurate dimension when being studied from postcritical theories such as poststructuralism, postcolonialism, postmodernism, post-Marxism, and posthumanism. Difference and particularity serve as a counterproposal to positions that understand the relationship between curriculum and society from universality, "otherwise, modernist theories will resemble 'a shrunken tight shirt' when trying to analyze and reflect upon contemporary educational matters" (Morelli, 2021c, p. 160). As Casimiro Lopes (2013) argues, "the post" implies problematizing schools of thought (such as structuralism, modernism, colonialism, Marxism, or humanism), giving way to the "particular demands and struggles of differences, of acceleration of cultural exchanges and global flows, of spatial-temporal compression" (Casimiro Lopes, 2013, p. 8). He also argues that this is neither a linear advance, an evolutionary advance, nor of epistemological improvement of those schools. Nor is there uniformity among them, since they often present contradictions regarding the way in which they understand the subject, the language, or the culture. To address curricular policies, enhance the concept of *Bildung*, and analyze the field of curriculum in Latin America in its hegemonic relationship with the United States, I turn to poststructuralism from Derrida's translation theory (1975, 2012, 2017), Laclau's discourse analysis (1993, 1996, 2005), and Mouffe's political theory (2005, 2009, 2012, 2014).

In addition to analyzing the state of the field of curriculum in Latin America from the perspective of postmodernism and poststructuralism, this text presents two other objectives. One of them aims to highlight the relationship between curriculum, didactics, and *Bildung*, admitting the lack of recognition of the latter in the region. The other objective analyzes the hegemony exercised by the United States as regards the conceptualization of curriculum in the rest of the continent. Although the exact date is unknown, the Latin American curriculum is being studied approximately since the beginning of the 21st century. Given the complexity of this object, this is a difficult task to saturate. The extension of its territories, the political diversities, the abundance of silenced stakeholders, and the immensity of hidden projects add up to the slowness shown by the unraveling of the Latin American curriculum. The topics that I deal with here are of my interest and have been studied for a little more than ten years. Even so, I do not intend to exhaust their treatment.

On the contrary, I intend to approach them with the partiality of one who looks at this field from Argentina, knowing some portions of the continent more than others. In my opinion, one of the concerns is linked to the hegemony received, which for many years conditioned the perspective with which curriculum theory and practices were understood.

This autobiographical introduction, which occupies the first part of the chapter, is followed by five other chapters. The second chapter, entitled "Constellations," is concerned with presenting the groups of curriculum scholars from Brazil and Mexico dedicated to postcritical theories in the field. There, I highlight the groups led, at present, by Elizabeth Macedo and Alice Casimiro Lopes, in the case of Brazil and by Alicia de Alba in Mexico. Guided by categories such as "influence" and "training," the constellations are academic groups that develop postcritical curriculum studies and, in my opinion, are two groups that articulate training in the rest of the Latin continent. The idea of constellation is not mine. I am inspired by an exhibition presented at the Museum of Modern Art (MoMA) in 2016 on the Japanese architect Toyo Ito and the influence exerted on a group of architects, some of them younger. This group of Japanese architects brought together by influence and training was called the "Japanese constellation" by curator Pedro Gadanho. Regarding the constellations formed by Brazil and Mexico, I would like to highlight the frameworks built for the field of curriculum from 1990 to the present, with emphasis on the passage from critical to postcritical theory and the legacy that these groups are leaving, in the present continuous, to the rest of the academics.

I could say that the third chapter, entitled "Translated Curriculum," presents three parts. One of them refers to curriculum policy theory, understood in the key of discourse as I have learned from Laclau and Mouffe (2010) and the Brazilian constellation. In the recognition of the curriculum as a text of politics, agonistics and translation become a (political) practice of reading and writing in different spheres of curricular decisions. Jacques Derrida considers that translation is an impossible task since the meaning of the text that initiates it is never exhausted, and the production of meaning is never guaranteed. In curricular policies, translation is a multiple, nonlinear production, and not from a first supra or macro-document to others. The second part features the teacher as a translator of the curriculum, through the possibility of elaborating their own texts in the field of school micro-politics. As if it were the missing link in the practice of curriculum policies, this is the most neglected aspect of this political process that offers the opportunity to do something different in and for a school. The particularity of each school institution marks an unbearable identity for the subjects that inhabit it, who generally prefer to adhere to the universality enunciated in documents at the macro- or meso-levels. The third part is devoted to the analysis of secondary school curriculum policies in Argentina, Brazil, Chile, and Mexico. Above all, I focus on categories that structure the Latin discourse for secondary education, such as "School

Trajectories" in the case of Argentina, "Life Project" for Brazil, and "Personal Project" for Mexico. These categories are proposed to alleviate the unresolved crisis at this level. As in the 1990s, once again, the resolution of a socio-educational problem such as the meaning of secondary school is channeled through the curricula. Installed as a slogan, at least in Argentina since 2006, "education as a right" is translated into curricular policies that obsessively emphasize what is common, pretending to guarantee the right to education of boys, girls, and young people. Like the best of national narratives, this is sealed in the vacuum of hegemony and does nothing more than reproduce universality so that this right reaches some and not all.

The following chapter, the fourth, is entitled "The promise of post-*Bildung*." In this chapter, I recover the concept of *Bildung*. Despite the criticisms of many of my colleagues for taking such a modern and Eurocentric concept that seems to have no place in Latin America, I believe in its power and in the possibility that it contains for something to happen in the education of young people in this part of the world. Deconstructing its meta-narrative, I come to elaborate it from a postcritical perspective, in order to address the special characteristics and differences. The challenge of post-*Bildung* proposes the elaboration of small narratives for the formation of a subject whose distinction and difference come from non-hegemonic logics, silenced by modern discourse. A subject whose intellectual identity needs to be defined from a perspective unrelated to the Enlightenment, one that involves their identity and sense of meaning as a Latin American. The conceptual ambiguity of *Bildung* allows us to recover the so-called *Bildung-centered Didaktik* for the field of school instruction and in it its relationship with the curriculum. My own training process related to this concept revolves around this chapter, in which I am interested in advancing in a postmodern conceptual construction that articulates curriculum-didaktik-*Bildung*.

"Why not America?," as a fifth chapter, is a calling for the awakening of America as a single continent from which its signifier (America) was taken away. Isn't the United States increasingly Latino? What does it mean to be American? Decolonizing (Latin) American curriculum studies implies deconstructing the hegemony that the United States has developed on the subject. Three events are identified for which the curriculum oscillates between cultural colonization and international emancipation: The first, when Latin America suffered the conceptual colonialism from 1970s to 1980s; once by the translation into Spanish with the importation of the United States' Technicist-Behavioral theory, enrolled in the *Alliance for Progress*; and then by the translations made by Spanish scholars from the Anglo-Saxon practical perspectives. That post-Franco's intervention in the Latin publishing market was like a second evangelization, five centuries later. The second event is given by the globalization and standardization of curriculum discourses in educational reforms led by multilateral organizations such as the World Bank and the Inter-American Development Bank in the 1990s. This colonization brings curriculum-based competencies and standardized assessments for education. For my understanding, with the creation of the PISA exams, Latin America only confirms the marginal space it occupies in a globalization scheme. Like a breath of fresh air, the third event shows the internationalization of curriculum studies from the 2000s. It arrives rejecting the idea of globalization and proposes the notion of curriculum as a complicated conversation, created by William Pinar (2012). In this way, the continent opened up the possibility of dialogue, in a double sense, inward and outward from America through solidarity ties that offered the possibility of collective constructions for the identity of the Latin American curriculum. In this chapter, I return to translation as a task that allowed the domination of the Latin. The selection, external and foreign, made by the Americans and the Spaniards about what to read in order to know the field of curriculum confirms once again the control over Latin America imposing a not very genuine course. This imposition has been present in the Latin American curriculum field and has conditioned it until the 2000s, when production slowly began to change, and asymmetries dissipated.

The sixth chapter, "Final Words," as a temporary conclusion, synthesizes the most important reflections contained in the previous chapters. The analyses carried out on the constellations formed by curriculum scholars' productions, the translations of the curriculum in a political key, the construction of the concept of post-*Bildung*, and the criticism of the hegemonic role of the United States over the rest of America are resumed. Is an attempt to recompose The Latino curriculum studies field. The situation is raised, but also suggestions to continue its study in future research.

I write this book with the eager desire to make visible curriculum studies in Latin America, from a perspective that places me in the south of the south. Sometimes I wonder if I am not looking upwards, where colonialism taught us to look, toward the north and looking for the center, with admiration for the unattainable. I immediately tell myself no, that I am looking at the continent from the place where I stand. From which, simultaneously I take distance and submerge myself in first person to feel it as my own and different from others. From Argentina, the country where my grandparents arrived trying to leave the European chaos between the wars, carrying in their trunks objects that accompanied me all my childhood and that I later found in the one-way trips that the curriculum granted me. From Argentina, a country that in 1884 sanctioned its first public, free, and secular Education Act, which managed to educate not only the children of immigrants who attended school but also their foreign parents, who became literate at the same pace as their children. A country that was once the beacon of Latin America, offering its inhabitants access to culture, education, health and social mobility. However, the wear and tear of dictatorships and the last 40 years of democracy have altered its former achievements. As a sample of the dregs of the world and of capitalist waste, today it is a country exploded by poverty, corruption, delinquency, social exclusion, and educational crisis. It is a country of multiple types of violence that merge with the other kinds of violence of the continent.

It is the curriculum studies that allow me to transform the pain and worry that this causes me. Writing means having something to say and bearing to make it public. It means communicating through editorial language ideas, questions, paradoxes, criticisms, and so on about the Latin curriculum. For Verón (1985), this task implies establishing a reading contract, where the text proposes its paths to the reader. As in a birth, once the book comes out and is in the hands of the readers, it no longer belongs to the author. New analyses, critiques, and new relationships will take place in the intellect of each reader and then this text will be deconstructed to become multiple texts by other authors, who will give them other meanings.

Note

1 The symposium was coordinated by Sean Wiebe (University of Prince Edward Island), Pamela Richardson (University of British Columbia), Diane Conrad (University of Alberta), Celeste Snowber (Simon Fraser University), Carl Leggo (University of British Columbia), Mitch McClarnon (University of Prince Edward Island), Karen Meyer (University of British Columbia), and Lyn Fels (Simon Fraser University). It took place on a school bus, as it traveled through the neighbourhoods of the city of Ottawa, simulating the routine that had taken us to school as children, familiar to all of us who were there.

2 Constellations

From March 13 to July 4, 2016, The Museum of Modern Art (MoMA) in New York City presented the exhibition *A Japanese Constellation: Toyo Ito, SANAA, and Beyond*, curated by Pedro Gadanho. In this exhibition, Gadanho highlights the influence of architect Toyo Ito on three generations of Japanese architects such as Kazuyo Sejima and Ryue Nishizawa (both from SANAA) and the young architects Sou Fujimoto, Akihisa Hirata, and Junya Ishigami.[1] According to its curator, the idea of constellation as a network of luminaries at work[2] is used and is "intended as a reflection on the transmission of an architectural sensibility and suggests an alternative model to what has been commonly described as an individuality-based 'star-system' in contemporary architecture."[3] Ito's influence on generations of architects is related to formation as a passage of experiences, theories, and practices. Like his colleagues, Ito demonstrates that a profession such as architecture requires as much care and sensitivity as the activity of design itself. Many of the works in question and of the encounters between these architects are set in motion after two events: the 1995 Kobe earthquake and The Great East Japan Earthquake of 2011 that caused the accident at the Fukushima nuclear power plant. It is striking to understand how the relationship with nature and the need to rebuild the country, caused by natural disasters, merges with an architectural notion that establishes links between these architects. Precisely when Gadanho evokes the constellation he places the emphasis on the crosses, links, and connections between them, rather than on highlighting the niches in which each performs. The non-hierarchical relationship between Ito and Sejima, Nishizawa, Fujimoto, Hirata, and Ishigami makes the notion of constellation reject the organization around centers within the stellar groups, distributing what the curator calls, as mentioned before, a network of luminaries in the work. A common language of structures, transparencies, luminosity, and a non-hierarchical distribution of the organization of space articulates the Japanese constellation. Ito's indelible mark, through formation and influence, can be found in the 44 projects that make up the exhibition.

I am interested in recovering the constellation as a metaphor to identify the configuration of curriculum studies in Latin America. These are consolidated

DOI: 10.4324/9781003475279-2

through events that foster intellectual conversations and creations that account for the growth of this field. Likewise, I recognize those who train others in topics specific to our region and influence those already trained or those at the beginning of their careers. To this end, I approach the constellations considering two key instances: one of them is the influence exerted by some academics, who stand out in the plot, and the other is formation as a pedagogical process of knowledge transmission. Pinar (2011c, pp. 3–4) for the case of curriculum studies in Mexico highlights the difference between preparation and formation and recovers the notion of formation linked to *Bildung* transmitted by Westbury et al. (2000/2015):

> Accordingly, then, instead of US-style "preparation" (as in teacher "preparation" or "training"), one finds in the chapters that follow references to "formation", a considerably more complex concept that recalls European conceptions of education, including *Didaktik* and *Bildung* (Westbury et al., 2000; Pinar, 2006). In contrast to the predominance of psychologism which in the United States has advanced a conception of individualism linked with capital accumulation and consumption and always focuses on "behavior", "formation" is a much more expansive and changing concept that integrates (but does not conflate) subjectivity and sociality.

In contrast to the American notion of "preparation/training," the notion of formation refers to a pedagogical process that focuses on the complementary and transferential link established between those who possess knowledge and those who wish to possess that knowledge. Recalling Pinar in what he mentions about the characteristics of formation and, as in the Japanese constellation, where the relationship between Ito and his colleagues has more to do with formation than with "preparation/training," I use this concept to refer to the processes in which knowledge is transmitted. The seduction that is exerted on another now of delivering knowledge is sustained by a relationship that is historical, subjective, and empathic, but above all asymmetrical, which needs to awaken fascination for the subject in question and admiration for the one who transmits it. The constellations are integrated by academic generations; by collaborations between other generations from other countries; by non-Latin influences and formations and by the institutions in which the groups are nucleated. I start by arguing that there is no intellectual field that does not engage with circumstances and that in this task groups of academics elaborate their notions of curriculum and their social participations articulated in what Pinar (2011a) calls a complicated conversation.

I believe that a complete book with many more authors' voices would be needed to deal with all the Latin American constellations. Therefore, in this chapter I will mention only two highly illuminated ones, shaped by local and foreign influences, which have allowed the formation of several generations, including my own. These are the Brazilian and Mexican groups. In view of the consolidation of postcritical curriculum theories, I will focus on a constellation influenced by Alicia de Alba, Alice Casimiro Lopes, and Elizabeth Macedo. Mexico and Brazil have a strong tradition in curriculum studies, being Mexico, before Brazil, the first country to have influenced the rest of the Latin American countries. While in Brazil the interest in curriculum studies starts in the 1950s, in Mexico it begins a decade later. The relevant characteristic of the latter is that it was a space for the formation of Latin American intellectuals, exiled during the dictatorships that struck the Latin American continent in the 1970s.

The groups in which Casimiro Lopes y Macedo and de Alba find themselves share the influence exerted by Ernesto Laclau and Chantal Mouffe (the latter especially in the Brazilian case). It should be noted that, in turn, the latter were influenced by the poststructuralist Jacques Derrida. With differences of a decade, Brazil enters poststructuralist studies in the 1990s while Mexico in the 2000s. In these constellations, the shift toward the postmodern made by these countries stands out and allows them to mark a path for Latin American theories and problems.

There are two events that should be highlighted that frame the work of both constellations. The first was William Pinar's keynote speech entitled "The Internationalization of Curriculum Studies" presented at the XII Congress of the Mexican Council for Educative Investigation (COMIE) in Guadalajara, in November 2003, where he presented the internationalization of the curriculum field through the creation of IAACS and enabled the circulation of productions and academics throughout the world. In this keynote, Pinar (2003b) postulates internationalization as opposed to globalization, the latter being installed as a phenomenon that tends toward uniformity and standardization, rejecting going "for new 'markets' for American conceptual products." Instead of this, he proposes, through internationalization, the invitation to interact between countries to share productions and meetings between academics. In his own words: "While internationalization supports transnational communication, it is important for each nation (and/or region) to cultivate its own 'indigenous' and conceptually independent curriculum theorizing, inquiry, and research" (Pinar, 2003b). While internationalization was being instituted among regions such as South Africa, India and Finland, Latin America began to identify itself as an area prone to internationalization, becoming visible as a forgotten part of the world. The second event is the Covid-19 pandemic, that poses a before and after (among other things), in the Latin American curriculum. The confinement and attachment to digital technologies exposes the social vulnerability and the difficulties to educate large parts of the population, especially regarding compulsory education. Despite this, the event-pandemic accelerates the processes of communication and formation between groups of the Latin American curriculum: a little because of the possibility of connectivity, as an exclusive means, and a little because of the need to support and accompany each other in such a critical moment. Conferences, Webinars, and academic meetings were developed nonstop during 2020 and 2021. After the end of the confinement, many proposals were consolidated in Brazil and Mexico, strengthening curricular studies in the region. The post-pandemic (Morelli, 2021a) includes these as challenges, reinstalling the concern for the curriculum-society relationship and technological change (de Alba, 2007, 2021) and the critique of the "myth of pedagogy" (Morelli, 2021b), produced by the subversion of the asymmetries between the knowledge of teachers and students.

The constellations of Mexico and Brazil are built with both foreign and local influences. They also present links between them. In addition to having achieved the advancement of curricular studies in their countries, they have offered formation processes in other Latin American constellations whose histories are more disruptive. I emphasize in these two groups the passage from critical Marxist theory to post-Marxist and poststructuralist theories in the construction of categories of analysis for curriculum theory. In philosophical terms, this passage is authorized by the so-called Modernity-postmodernity tension (Morelli, 2016, p. 29) expressed through the debate between Jürgen Habermas and Jean-François Lyotard after the appearance of *The Postmodern Condition*, in 1979, written by the latter. As an example of this, it is worth recalling the passage of Alicia de Alba (1995, pp. 59–74) from her so-called "notion of curriculum" in which she explains that the curriculum is a dialectical synthesis composed of a political-educational proposal. She states that the curriculum is made up of hegemonic and counter-hegemonic elements, presenting the possibility of negotiations between sectors with different interests. All this process framed in an institutional environment and with a historical nature. In the lecture given at the Fourth IAACS Conference of 2012, held in the city of Rio de Janeiro, entitled *El curriculum como dispositivo educativo de poder-saber y voluntad poder y de ser. Una lectura político-educativa a partir de Laclau y Foucault* (The curriculum as an educational device of power-knowledge and will power and being. A political-educational reading from Laclau and Foucault) de Alba continues his notion of curriculum. This time, from a discursive and postmodern perspective, she mentions the curriculum as a device of knowledge-power (Morelli, 2016, p. 36) introducing the category of "social contour" and mentioning the equivalential chain, derived from Ernesto Laclau's Discourse Theory. A similar case occurs with curriculum studies in Brazil. Casimiro Lopes and Macedo (2014, p. 93) argue that "until the mid-1990s, critical thinking was strongly hegemonic in curriculum theory and policy in Brazil" and that this Marxist hegemony begins to wane with the incorporation of a poststructuralist perspective. Even so, there are still remnants of Marxism in the curriculum when considering the concepts of "subject, emancipation and equality" and the idea of "crisis as an engine of change" (Casimiro Lopes and Macedo, 2014, p. 94).

Influence and formation

The Brazilian constellation has two academics who, it could be said, exert influence on those who study postcritical theories. Between Antonio Flavio Moreira of the Federal University of Rio de Janeiro (UFRJ) and Tomaz Tadeu da Silva of the Federal University of Rio Grande do Sul (UFRGS) is the passage from critical curriculum theory to postmodern perspectives. In the case of Moreira, with a direct influence on Casimiro Lopes and Macedo, both from the State University of Rio de Janeiro (UERJ), he made contributions to the theory and history of curriculum and multiculturalism, establishing the relationship between curriculum, culture, and difference. His postgraduate formation, both for doctorate and post-doctorate, was at the University of London, influenced by Michael Young, bringing critical English curricular notions to the Brazilian context. This contribution can be seen in the studies conducted by Casimiro Lopes and Macedo (2011) on disciplinarity and school knowledge. For this group, the study of Young (1981, 1989, 2000) on the new sociology of education, for the sociological construction of school knowledge and Ball's studies on curriculum policies by recontextualization through hybridism (see Casimiro Lopes et al., 2011, 2013) have been very fruitful.

Tomaz Tadeu da Silva also departs from a Marxist notion to study the field of curriculum, deepening the critique of the modern school from postmodern and poststructuralist perspectives. Unlike Moreira, he emphasizes the subject and identity as the two problems of Modernity, although he poses them as small narratives, resisting the grand narrative. He recognizes the decentering of the subject of Modernity (Silva, 1997, 1999) whom he highlights as "the greatest victim" in the crisis of the modern school. To refer to discourse, he recovers contributions from Foucault, in the relation knowledge-power and from Derrida, in the deconstruction of its relationship with language and the abandonment of structures. The influence of Moreira and Silva on Casimiro Lopes and Macedo can be seen both in the passage from the Marxist perspective to the postcritical ones and in the adoption of poststructuralism to address the relationship between curriculum and discourse, multiculturalism, and difference. Thus, in the presentation of the book *Teorias de currículo* Alice Casimiro Lopes and Elizabeth Macedo call the contributions received from Silva and Moreira that made this book possible "secret references." In short, they are nothing more than those translucent but indelible marks that are transmitted by those who have been involved in their formation. In an autobiographical manner, the authors argue that "The books *Curriculos e programas no Brasil*, by A.F. Moreira and *Documentos de identidade*, by T.T. da Silva, as well as an introduction by both to *Currículos, cultura e sociedade* are part of these secret references" (Casimiro Lopes and Macedo, 2011, p. 16).

The University of Essex intervenes influencing the Brazilian and Mexican constellations through Ernesto Laclau and Chantal Mouffe confirming the study of discourse theory in the curriculum. They also guarantee the arrival of poststructuralism through Jacques Derrida, who, in turn, exerts his influence over them. It should also be noted that both the Brazilian and Mexican groups, prior to the arrival of Derrida, carried out studies on Foucault's poststructuralism, a task that they brought to the educational field. As a key piece in the Brazilian and Mexican constellations, Laclau contributes, in the case of the former, the critical reading of Marxism. The passage to postmodern and poststructuralist perspectives is complemented by what was initiated by Moreira and Silva, although it should be noted that it is consolidated with the discourse theory of Laclau and Mouffe (see Laclau, 1993, 1996, 2005; Laclau and Mouffe, 2010). This is evidenced in the use of the categories of discourse, articulation, and difference, as well as in political categories such as hegemony, democracy and conflict. The Laclau-Mouffe binomial is enhanced when the Brazilian constellation enters poststructuralism by taking Derrida's (1975, 2012, 2017) translation and deconstruction as a language to understand the curriculum politically. This is the line printed by Casimiro Lopes and Macedo in Graduate Program in Education (PROPED) at UERJ. Curriculum policies are understood as a discursive and undecidable construction, lacking fixed rules and unpredictable. This position considers educational practices and subjects in their particularities and differences. Macedo adds to the poststructuralist approach the postcolonial perspective that allows understanding "another individual from the optics of the notion of time, little problematized in curricular theory" (Macedo, 2018, p. 155).

The influence of Laclau and Mouffe in the Mexican constellation begins to be noticed in the studies carried out by de Alba (2007), which allows the author to create the category of Generalized Structural Crisis (CEG, *Crisis Estructural Generalizada*), the relationship between social subjects and education, and to consider Lyotard's (2004/1979) critique of scientific knowledge. In my opinion, the pandemic scenarios confirmed that we were living what de Alba calls CEG, adding to this the notion of "technological change" where de Alba (2021) analyzes the place of digital technologies in the virtual scenarios of the pandemic. This last approach enriches it by placing under suspicion the antagonism of the face-to-face-virtuality relationship.

The Brazilian constellation becomes deep, when it branches out to Rosanne Evangelista Dias (2011, 2019; Evangelista Dias et al., 2011, 2023), from postcritical studies of teacher training and Rita Frangella (2018; Ramos and Frangella, 2014; Oliveira and Frangella, 2022) studying school and literacy in compulsory education. A recent generation is that of Talita Vidal Pereira (2021; Ramahlo Ortigão and Vidal Periera, 2019), Thiago Ranniery (Ranniery and Macedo, 2018; Scofano Medieros and Ranniery, 2018) and Hugo Camilo Costa (2021; Camilo Costa and Casimiro Lopes, 2011). Distributed among Casmiro Lopes, Macedo, Dias Evangelista, Frangella and Vidal Pereira, about 30 doctoral and postdoctoral fellows, based at UERJ, coming from different corners of Brazil, continue with these studies. Thus, curricular designs for compulsory education, the study of school disciplines, evaluation and progress in curricular theory are covered from specific categories of discourse theory that approach curricular studies from a postmodern perspective.

The density of the Mexican constellation has been growing steadily since the early 1970s. Although at the beginning it was Raquel Glazman and María de Ibarrola (Pinar, 2011c) who made the curriculum visible through *Design of Study Plan*, it was Ángel Díaz Barriga who influenced the rest of the academics, dealing with the formation of groups since the early 1980s. This author's involvement with the field is noticeable in the studies on curricular theory and its relationship with didactics, the school anchoring of the curriculum, teacher training and evaluation (of the learnings, the curriculum, the university curriculum). In Alicia de Alba, Concepción Barrón Tirado, Frida Díaz Barriga Arceo and José María García Garduño are evident the "indelible marks" of Díaz Barriga as an educator (see Pinar, 2011c). Successive generations demonstrate a broad and polysemic field capable of dealing with epistemological and philosophical aspects, curriculum development, evaluation, disciplinary or interdisciplinary relations for the presentation of knowledge, university curriculum, flexible curriculum, curriculum by competencies. In an attempt to materialize the constellations, I argue that the Brazilian constellation has delimited borders and is profound, while the Mexican constellation has permeable borders (inside and outside the country) and comprises a wider range of topics.

Another indelible mark is left by Alicia de Alba, with her adherence to postmodern perspectives. Laclau and Mouffe's discourse analysis, in the Mexican case, was capitalized to produce contributions to the post-pandemic curriculum (de Alba, 2021). This marked a movement of the Mexican group that permeates the boundaries between critical theory and postcriticism, focusing on curriculum studies in situations of virtuality, isolation, educational abandonment, as problems presented by the suspension of materiality (Morelli, 2021b). The group belongs to the University and Education Research Institute (IISUE) of the National Autonomous University of Mexico (UNAM) and includes, in addition to Ángel Díaz Barriga and Alicia de Alba, Bertha Orozco Fuentes (2015, 2020), Concepción Barrón Tirado (2020; Díaz Barriga-Arceo and Barrón Tirado, 2020, 2022, 2023); Lourdes Chehaibar (2020). Ana Gallardo Gutiérrez leads the way for a later generation. All of them have gone through the influence of de Alba and Díaz Barriga. From Laclau's discourse theory and from postcolonialism Gallardo Gutiérrez (2015, 2017, 2021) makes a valuable contribution to the interculturality of the Mexican curriculum. Outside of the IISUE, but at UNAM, Frida Díaz Barriga-Arceo (Díaz-Barriga-Arceo et al., 2022, Coll Salvador et al., 2023) focuses on curriculum development with digital technological mediations, highlighting the role of both teachers and students, during and after the pandemic. It should be noted that this author strengthens the links of this constellation with Barrón Tirado. Another author within the Mexico City orbit, although from the Autonomous University of Mexico City (UACM), is García Garduño. This author, like de

Alba, introduces Pinar into Mexican curricular studies, translating him into Latin American languages. In *La teoría del curriculum* (Pinar, 2014b) García Garduño (2014), in addition to selecting works by Pinar, carries out what he himself calls "Introductory Study" carrying out a complete introduction to the curricular theory of William Pinar.

Outside the orbit of UNAM, at the Autonomous University of San Luis Potosí (UASLP), Rita Angulo Villanueva is part of the expanding constellation. Angulo Villanueva's studies are based on political discourse analysis. In a recent study, for post-pandemic contexts she creates the category of Emerging Curriculum Code (CCE, *Código Curricular Emergente*) (Angulo Villanueva, 2022; Angulo Villanueva et al., 2023). Based on Lundgren's (1991) notion of Curriculum Code, it recovers for classroom work knowledge that is not part of the official curriculum. Understanding the pandemic as an "event" and as "contingent," she takes up from Badiou (2011a) and Laclau and Mouffe (2010) the construction of other itineraries for the practices of Mexican and Latin American education after Covid-19. In Zacatecas (UAZ) Manuel Martínez Delgado, inspired by a poststructuralist Foucault, is concerned with deepening biographical and autobiographical studies of teachers (Martínez Delgado, 2015). In the State of Mexico, David Pérez Arenas (2021) makes onto-epistemological contributions to think "the pedagogical and critical thinking, in the conformation of new social identities according to current contexts" such as those of the post-pandemic. A recent work coordinated by Barrón Tirado (2023) on new subjectivities and technologies in the curriculum offers debates on the articulation between school, curriculum, and ICT after the Covid-19 pandemic. With a foreword by de Alba, Orozco Fuentes, Glazman Nowalski, Furlán and Eli Ochoa, Gallardo Gutiérrez, Angulo-Villanueva and Reducindo-Ruiz, Díaz Barriga Arceo and López Banda, and Heredia Sánchez collaborate by offering ideas on this issue. As a disruptive and discursive event (Barrón Tirado, 2023) the pandemic proposes to the subject other ways of attending school through technologies. In this production, the work of Gallardo Gutiérrez (2023) is positioned from the productions of the Latin American Seminar curriculum derived from the polyphony of voices of Mexican academics. Gallardo Gutiérrez positions herself in the interstices produced by this seminar to recognize a new digital subjectivity. Under the dispersion and differentiation of projects that mark the curriculum-society relationship the author highlights:

> At the same time, we also note the erosion of such neoliberal policies and the emergence of contentious discourses coming from contemporary social movements centered on gender, intercultural and environmental issues, although neoconservative and radical right-wing discourses also emerge as new forms of fascism that threaten to further destabilize contemporary societies.
>
> (Gallardo Gutiérrez, 2023, pp. 135–136)

Meanwhile, Angulo-Villanueva and Reducindo-Ruiz (2023) refer to the subjects of curricular overdetermination in a sick society. Highlighting the construction of new hyperconnected subjectivities in the worlds of young people, since the pandemic new discourses emerge in Latin America.

> When there is some signifier that summons and organizes them and generates interest, a rhizome is constituted (for example, gender groups: women-only, men-only, LGBTQ+) that welcomes within it many multiplicities (characters, backgrounds, purposes, personalities), many connections (family, political, academic) and the yearning for a certain takeover of power (for example, the impulse to feminism as a way to protest against violence towards women from the Chilean performance *El violador eres tú* [You are the rapist]; Las Tesis, 2019).
>
> (Angulo-Villanueva y Reducindo-Ruiz, 2023, p. 164)

For the authors, technological mediation, and the construction of new subjectivities in the school affect both the teacher and the student, creating new narratives for the curriculum.

I must emphasize that the Brazilian and Mexican groups maintain a dialogue that, according to Pinar (2014a), can be recognized as a complicated conversation. The curricular dialogues between these groups (Casimiro Lopes and de Alba, 2014; de Alba and Casimiro Lopes, 2015) are amalgamated by common theories and shared categories, but also by assumed differences. There are three important moments in this dialogue; the first one is the edition of *Curriculum Studies in Mexico. Intellectual Histories, Present Circumstances* (Pinar, 2011c) in which Casimiro Lopes participated as a commentator, the second one is the Fourth Theoretical Turns International Meeting: Language, Transgression and Borders (*IV Encuentro Internacional Giros Teóricos: Lenguaje, transgresión y fronteras*), in February 2012 in Mexico City and the third one is the "Fourth IAACS Congress," in July 2012 in Rio de Janeiro. This dialogue, which began in 2011, not only reaches academics from both countries, but also spreads among other Latin American groups. Institutional and academic consistency is experienced as a possibility for the rest of the countries that approach to both constellations influenced by postcritical approaches or seeking formation. A synthesis that highlights the Mexican constellation is the Latin American Curriculum Seminar (*Seminario Curriculum Latinoamericano*). Organized at IISUE, developed in a hybrid technological format since 2018, it is an inter-institutional space, which contemplates the internationalization of the curriculum field. Its hybrid characteristic allows it to survive in pandemic when the monthly meetings were carried out online. But I would like to highlight the hybridity with which the space is created. With stable academics such as Alicia de Alba, Bertha Orozco, Concepción Barrón, Rita Angulo and Ana Gallardo Gutiérrez, it offers intersections with other Latin American professors where issues regarding curriculum theory in Latin America or specific to each context are addressed. It also deals with problems of educational practice or curriculum policies of different Latin American sectors. From a formation perspective, this seminar is a place for academic debate and for postgraduate training, as it is attended by scholarship holders and master's and doctoral thesis students.

The meeting between Mexico and Brazil (in addition to Argentina and Chile) merges into the creation, in December 2023, of the "Red latinoamericana de estudios curriculares" (*Latin American Network of Curriculum Studies*). As an incipient space, it promises to strengthen the groups in the region by consolidating the academic task, which would cease to be segmented and would favor the construction of a regional identity. The tension between similarities, meeting points and differences between contexts are the key to the network, whose horizon is loaded with projects and promises. This tension seeks the solidarity necessary to generate a boost in curricular studies in Latin America.

Contributions of constellations

In contexts such as the one of Latin America, academic productions make no sense if there is no impact on the critical problems arising from circumstances and contingencies. Without forgetting that most of the universities are national, this generates a greater commitment with the management of the public and social sectors. From this approach, it is important to identify contributions to curricular problems. Under the notion of "network of luminaries at work," this chapter identifies scholars within these constellations and their conceptual contributions to the Latin American curriculum in the passage from critical to postcritical theories, in the treatment of postmodern, postcolonial, and poststructuralist categories and in the re-edification of the curriculum in the post-pandemic. According to the groups studied, I highlight four concepts that I consider relevant: hybridism, culture, difference, and technological change.

Hybridism

Hybridism is recovered by García Garduño for Latin American curriculum studies. With the metaphor of *mestizaje* (mix of races) García Canclini, quoted by García Garduño (2011), refers to hybridity as an anthropological category. For the latter, "Latin America is a living example of hybridity" (García Garduño, 2011, p. 141). It is worth saying that a hybridization is the complementary combination – sometimes random, sometimes planned – of structures that, when they meet, form something new and unprecedented, even weird, because of the occurrence of the unusual and the unknown. A hybrid construction can be uncomfortable and uncommon. García Garduño himself argues that in Latin America the *Spanglish* is the most evident hybridization of speech developed by Latinos in the United States and Canada. To this I add *Portuñol*, which is the mixture of Portuguese and Spanish languages (originated in the triple border between Argentina, Brazil, and Uruguay), which also helps communication in these countries. Likewise, Casimiro Lopes (2011, p. 125) refers to hybridity as the loss of a common language and the accumulation of knowledge. Considering it through the metaphor of libraries, for the cultural compilation, he proposes to value its canons without this implying to support the belief of identities as fixed entities. He understands hybridism as a category to rethink the stability with which history is constructed. In epistemological terms, curricular studies in Brazil tension, with hybrid parameters, the relationship between disciplinarity and transdisciplinarity in the study of subjects.

Hybridity, in contemporary post-pandemic curriculum studies, has the possibility of creating an intermediate space of mixtures that allows the approach to the unexpected, created from contingency and randomness. For curricular studies in Brazil, Pinar (2011a, 2011b) sustains hybridity according to what Wang (2004) calls "in between" or "third space," as an autobiographical journey in which the subject must deal with himself and with otherness. But also, according to García Canclini (2007), hybridity is a bridge that cushions the passage from the modern to the postmodern, that can be identified as a cultural reconciliation. Not between antagonistic cultures but rather between cultural fragments, modern and postmodern, of those usually found in the curriculum. The author argues:

> Today we conceive Latin America as a more complex articulation of traditions and modernities (diverse, unequal), a heterogeneous continent formed by countries where, in each one, multiple logics of development coexist. To rethink this heterogeneity, the anti-evolutionary reflection of postmodernism, more radical than any previous one, is useful.
>
> (García Canclini, 2007, p. 43)

The technological hybridity exposed in the pandemic revives this debate where the modern origin of the school and the curriculum, the pedagogical relationship and the technology inscribed in the didactic scene are questioned. As a literacy metaphor, digital technologies enable us to rely on hybridity as a new meaning for the literacy process. It is natural to think of it as a mixture between presentiality and virtuality, but according to García Canclini (2007, p. 260) the potential of this notion requires three key processes: the breakdown and mixing of the collections that organize cultural systems, the deterritorialization of symbolic processes and the expansion of impure genres. A conceptual anchorage that sustains hybridity allows Latin American post-pandemic curricula to build other perspectives from which to approach the school class, micro-political decisions, the identity of subjects and all that, unforeseen, that relates to new cultural systems, deterritorialization and impure genres.

Culture

The internationalization of the curriculum and the passage from critical to postcritical theories allows Latin American regions to identify minorities in an incessant process that requires the formation of groups, adherence to theories, identification of categories, while the spectrum of minorities broadens. In my opinion, when referring to minorities, it is not meant that they are small groups in number, but that the characteristic of minority is given by the socio-cultural indifference to the problems they denounce and the lack of visibility as social groups. Thus, feminism, blackness, disability, indigenism, LGBTQI+ groups and ethnic and linguistic diversities began to raise their voices and to shape their groups.

It is the works of Ana Gallardo Gutiérrez and Elizabeth Macedo that make the most significant contributions where culture is treated in a broad sense, not reducing culture to manifestations and lifestyles, but taking the debate to the articulation with the political. Macedo (2021, pp. 133–134) argues that "the conservative inflection is not only materialized in the field of economy, but also in the spheres of political representation and culture." An event that stresses interculturality is the frequent migrations between countries in the Americas. Gallardo Gutiérrez (2021, p. 191) considers Mexico an "ethnic, cultural and linguistic diversity." Encapsulated in macro policies under the denomination of "mestizos," racism is disguised, leaving out native peoples and Afro-Americans. She also warns that the flow of migrations, throughout the history of America, creates new interculturalities that deserve to be considered in the curricula. In another text (Gallardo Gutiérrez, 2015, pp. 66–67), citing Schemelkes (2009), she emphasizes that the lack of ethnic, cultural, and linguistic relevance of schooling shows that there are groups that need to "compensate" their differences to access the educational system. Having noticed this problem in Mexico, Intercultural Bilingual Education (EIB, *Educación Intercultural Bilingüe*) was institutionalized to understand cultural diversity based on the indigenous movement, although in opposition to the Mexican reality. The author argues that, after the Zapatista National Liberation Movement, cultural diversity was assumed in the country for all the inhabitants of the Republic. When she focuses on this problem in Latin America, she says that:

> Diversity in Latin American countries alludes to the processes of colonization and miscegenation that have not been resolved in the construction of a homogeneous national identity that does not respond to the cultural conformation of Latin American countries, as is the case of Mexico.
>
> (Gallardo Gutiérrez, 2015, p. 67)

Macedo (2015, p. 83) argues that in the 1990s the Brazilian curriculum begins to foster postmodern and poststructuralist debates with discourses focused on language, culture, and difference. It resists the notion of culture as something that must be taught, adding to it the power relations that define the value of what must be taught. However, a postmodern interpretation of the concept of culture highlights the sense of belonging experienced by the subjects toward cultural groups, their identities being "multifaceted, changing, fluid, often articulating values in conflict with each other" (Macedo, 2015, p. 87). Citing Appadurai (2001), she agrees that "the cultural" is nothing more than systems of meanings that institute sense, being a cultural practice, equivalent to the notion of discursive practice, never concluded.

Gallardo Gutiérrez (2015, p. 71), taking the notion of curriculum proposed by de Alba (1995), who considered the "cultural synthesis," refers to the intercultural curriculum as that constructed by the articulation of knowledge, wisdom and values that account for this synthesis. For the author, this notion of curriculum forces us to think of a common curriculum from the particular and local, as opposed to the "adaptation" of the local to national norms. To this end, she recovers from de Alba (2007) the notion of "cultural contact" as the staging of an intercultural relationship characterized by inequality, conflict, and the production of new identities (Gallardo Gutiérrez, 2015, p. 75). Cultural contact makes it possible to recognize, know and value diversity. Likewise, she warns of two dangers, one is the idea of the local as the preservation of what is our own, leading to self-segregation, and the other is the perpetuation of relations of domination with the consequent marginalization of native Mexican cultures.

Difference

This is probably one of the categories around which the Brazilian constellation is organized, which lean toward the notion of culture and conflicts with the concept of "common curriculum," which will be discussed in the next chapter. Taking contributions from Laclau (2008) and Derrida (2012) they manage to elaborate a framework for understanding difference as a problem of the curriculum. Both Macedo and Casimiro Lopes think of difference in the relationship between the curriculum and the political. This not only institutes particular identity, but also assumes the non-predictability of events, the argument that all difference is political and the lack of a center of domination. Macedo and Tomé (2018, p. 11) also highlight the effort to bring out the meaning of difference. They argue that "difference" is being suffocated by the specter of equality and diverse identities. When the authors refer to this, they are making it clear that they are starting from a notion of difference that is not synonymous with diversity, although neither is it antagonistic to equality. For Macedo (2015, p. 83) equality and difference have their own political dynamics that cannot be analyzed in a generic way. Contingency is always involved in them. The concept of difference arises from the recognition of identity demands, when small multicultural voices demand recognition, while establishing commitment to otherness. Moreover, it is encouraging to note the articulation contained in this concept when, rejecting a notion of individuality that an unsuspecting reader might associate with it, it relates to Wang's (2004) "in between" or "third space," rescued in this chapter from a quote by Pinar (2011a, 2011b). This highlights that difference is derived from hybridity, and, at the same time, the recognition of hybrid constructions enables the creation of different "identities."

It is worth remembering that as a category of analysis "difference" was created by Derrida in 1967, a year before the political and social effervescence that would lead to emancipation paths as regards sexuality, political practices, women, gays and lesbians (Asensi Pérez, 2012). This allows us to think of difference as a term that inscribes the presence of others, who are part of the complexity and contingency of the curriculum. Difference makes visible the particularity of the subjects, enabling them through writing. It is worth saying that, in the presence of language, this is translated into writing to give entity to the difference. Macedo (2015) states that this is a category constructed by language since there is never a difference *a priori*, but rather from that which is labeled as different.

Technological change

In 2007, de Alba wondered why technological change is still in many cases absent in the field of curriculum. This is a concern that the author brings with postcritical theories to scenarios in which literacy merges with ICT and virtuality. In this way, she poses what she calls technological change in the relationship between curriculum-science and technology. Oriented by Lyotard's postmodern condition, she takes up his notion of curriculum, understood as a political and cultural synthesis to understand the production and transfer of knowledge. Likewise, influenced by Edgar Morin (2001), she constructs a notion of complex curriculum that implies new learning, new literacies, the incorporation of older generations and dialogues (de Alba, 2007, p. 191). A contribution foreign to the field of curriculum, but not to that of Mexican educational research is made by Rosa Nidia Buenfil (1995), resorting to postmodern characteristics to think about technological change. She proposes:

> … relationalism; the floating character of the sign; the floating or sliding character of frontiers; the open character of configurations; the impossibility of establishing an ultimate foundation for ontological, political, ethical and aesthetic epistemological proposals; the critique of fixed centers; the critique of globalizing, universalizing theories and political strategies; the critique of the transcendental, unidimensional, teleological, universal, sutured and centered subject; the impossibility of apprehending the real through form, thought or reason; the impossibility of apprehending the

> totality of beings through thought; the incompleteness of all confirmation, and the constitutive character of contingency in the formation of processes.
>
> (de Alba, 2007, p. 200)

This postmodern framework elaborated by the author and applied by de Alba to technological change shows similarities with the Brazilian constellation, which coincides with Buenfil's theoretical assumptions, and at the same time it should be noted that both de Alba, the Brazilian constellation and Buenfil share the influence of Laclau for the configuration of postmodern ideas.

A problem highlighted by de Alba (2021) in technological change concerning the relationship between curriculum-science and technology is the constitution of new social subjects in the inclusion of technologies, which leads to exclusion, in the opposite side. According to the author, the conformation of new social spaces, with different materialities, created by technological change, enables another notion of subject referred to by the author as "online/offline." The social marginality of the subject who has become an educator, student, researcher, or specialist forces us to redefine him/her as included in the new social spaces, created in the hybridity left by the pandemic. Returning to the category of cultural contact, this also intervenes in the definition of the postmodern online/offline subject.

Notes

1 Amanda Reeser Lawrence (see Lawrence, 2016) highlights that Gadanho did not take into account, as part of the constellations, three engineers: Cecil Balmond, Mutsuro Sasaki, and Masato Araya, highlighted in a scheme elaborated by Ito, entitled "Ito and the surroundings". The observation not only adds the names that Lawrence believes are missing from the constellation, but also highlights Ito's view of the complementarity between architecture and engineering.

2 https://www.moma.org/calendar/exhibitions/1615.

3 https://www.moma.org/calendar/exhibitions/1615.

3 Translated curriculum

To address curriculum policies in this chapter, I begin by recognizing the conceptual ambiguity of the curriculum by considering it, as Lundgren (1991) argues, as a text in context that attempts to solve the problem of representation. From a discourse perspective, curriculum policies are understood as the construction of a text with political meaning, in which its semiosis is more prominent than its semantics. In other words, priority is given to the chosen ways of saying rather than to the content of what is said. In the curricular tradition, technical perspectives have taught to simplify curricular policies, inscribing them in the administrative sphere. However, by considering them in terms of discourse, the construction of meanings used by and to elaborate curricular text is identified. In the difficult and sometimes contradictory relationship between the levels of curricular policies, there are passages where they are transformed. This is where it is worth considering what Derrida (2017, p. 23) says when he argues that "things change from one context to another." This means that each level of curriculum policy presents its differences, due to the field it represents, and that they are also combined with the particularities and circumstances of each context. But each time a curriculum policy moves from one level to another, it will undergo changes that are accompanied by conflict.

Identifying the particularities of change, translation is recognized as a philosophy of intellection and political practice to understand the meanings given to curricular tasks. I start by considering Derrida's (1975, 2012, 2017) theory on translation, which understands it in relation to writing and deconstruction. It is already known that no text is spared from being translated. Once the subjects of the curriculum come into contact with this practice in a political sense, varied senses are possible to be elaborated. This task carries the illusion that the language produced as a target of the translation constructs a new text that does not dissociate the meaning of the translated text. However, it should be noted that it is impossible to avoid this dissociation, besides the fact that the meaning that the translation constructs is always partial and is not saturated by any of the translations. In other words, translation is never

DOI: 10.4324/9781003475279-3

complete and there is always the possibility of constructing new, unforeseen, unexpected meanings that are far from the source texts. Regarding the latter, the origin of the text being translated is questioned, asking where it begins. Even if it is the first time that it is part of a written text, its "origin" is always doubtful, since before being written it was a practice or idea. Questioning its originality, every time a text is translated it triggers countless productions of meaning. This shows that the curriculum, as a written text, was previously a socio-educational practice or comes from another written text.

In curriculum policies, translation is never linear, not even from one document to another. Rather, it is a multiple translation. If we take the case of Argentina, translating from macro-policy to mesopolitics will bring into play 24 different translations that correspond to the jurisdictions in which the curriculum is organized (23 provinces and the autonomous city of Buenos Aires). Although all of them are translating the same curriculum policy generated at the national level by the Federal Council of Education (CFE, *Consejo Federal de Educación*), they may present theoretical, cultural, didactic and administrative differences among them, which are synthesized in definitions of what Mouffe (2009) calls "politics" and "political,"[1] and even so, they still refer to national agreements regarding what to consider in the curriculum. Therefore, it will not cease to be the Argentine curriculum because it has 24 different ways of being considered.

Derrida (2017) argues that translation is an impossible task and there is never fidelity to the source text, which is always betrayed for political, theoretical, cultural or practical reasons. This allows us to understand that, just as every curricular document is translated, none of its translations manages to come up with a complete idea of the text, while imprinting other meanings on it. The "betrayal" that confirms the lack of fidelity entails the possibility of creating new and particular meanings to the text, according to the subjects of the curriculum, their identities and contexts. This is why the trust in the legitimacy of the origin of a text is discarded, casting doubt on it for considering it random and relative. This makes translation suspicious and impossible, but inevitable. Since every translated text comes from another translation, it is pertinent to recognize the incessant process of translations to which any curricular text is subjected. The insistence on adhering to the source and seeking fidelity gives rise to myth. It means that the naivety of recognizing a text as the original distances it from new constructions of meaning offered by translation and, as Derrida (1975, p. 109) affirms, "repeats itself without knowing." Myth is a narrative stripped of time and space, revered for its validity and universality (Morelli, 2021a). The depoliticized subjects of the myth are reduced to alienated characters of the curricular circumstances. They grant criteria of truth to a text that can only be justified through the illusion of control over the meaning of the text, assuming that in different circumstances the translation will not vary. The myth has the technicist ideal of denying the particularity of practices, pretending that a source text determines the curricular spheres.

Immersed in his own alienation, the depoliticized subject does not realize their participation in the elaboration of the curricular text, preventing themselves to betray the meaning and submitting themselves to the determination of a text whose meaning was constructed externally.

There is no translation without deconstruction, says Derrida and asks "what is not deconstruction? what should it not be?" (Derrida, 2017, pp. 23, 25). For the author, in deconstruction "it is a matter of undoing, of decomposing, of disedimenting structures." But a translation is the deconstruction of something particular, since the universal (Badiou, 2011a, p. 31), would not resist it. In Derrida's terms, a text is deconstructed as long as it has the materiality granted by writing, which is the writing of the particular. Regarding writing, Derrida (2012) argues that it is something more than a tool of speech, although it has been understood as its supplement, which led it to have a secondary and corollary function to that which was spoken. In the differentiation between orality and writing, the author proposes to understand the latter as a deconstruction of the criterion of truth granted to logocentrism. Thus, the translation of a curricular text is the deconstruction of the criterion of truth contained in the text from which it is translated.

In curricular policies, it is important to recognize translation through deconstruction as a process of rewriting that resists its hegemonic condition. Nothing is more alienating than to install the myth of universality stripped of the materiality of writing that represents a subject and its circumstances in democracy. The object of curricular policies is none other than the conditions in which the subject, as a citizen and political subject, is educated. Curricular policies make evident the decisions considered for subjects in particular societies. In this way, an indispensable relationship between them is highlighted, proposed by the tension between hegemony and democracy. Following Mouffe's (2005, p. 16) analysis regarding deconstruction and Derrida's theory, the author argues that deconstruction requires a theory of hegemony, that is, a theory about decision-making in the terrain of the undecidable. In turn, Laclau (2005, p. 97) argues that hegemony is a central category for the theorization of politics. When curricular policies are understood from the perspective of deconstruction, they deal with the achievement of agreements as a temporary result of a provisional hegemony. Because, ultimately, on the horizon of curriculum policies is the design of a democratic policy that involves the education of the subjects of the curriculum.

Badiou (2011b, p. 127) states that a deconstruction does not admit antagonisms, pitting one idea against another. Rather, deconstruction is a transversality that includes several positions, while remembering that it possesses a vanishing point (Badiou, 2011b, p. 127). That is to say, a point that flees from the rule of the imposing device. What would be a vanishing point in the decisions of the curriculum if not that which escapes from determination and which appears as the unthought, the unimagined that becomes possible. It can be recognized as the alternative that takes into account the particularity of the circumstances and the subjects. In short, in the vanishing point we find the construction of unexpected meanings, enabled by the betrayal to the translated text.

Teachers as translators at school

When reference is made to the political organization of the curriculum, it is very common to recover it through the supra, macro, micro, meso, and nano levels. In my opinion, the problem is not how to delimit what each level contains and how it differs from the others, but rather how they relate to each other and at what level the political process of translation is noticed. In the classic organization of curricular policies, two methods are as well-known as they are applied. The one that establishes translations from the top (supra level) to the bottom (nano level) and the one that translates from the bottom (nano level) to the top (supra level). The first corresponds to *Tyler Rationale*'s technicist model, which seeks to control practice by assuming the homogeneity of schools and classrooms, while the second is an emancipatory critical model that seeks macro-political determination from the school class. Either of the two models demands linearity and entails the illusion of the myth to control the other one. Either of the two models requires the obligatory passage through each of the levels of curricular policy, because if this does not occur, the other extreme would never be reached. Rejecting antagonism as dichotomous, I believe that the political process of the curriculum can be noticed at any level, without the need to follow a linear process. That is to say, it can be noticed from the interstice left by the friction between politics and the political. Positioned beyond antagonism, I note that it is the micro level which, due to its characteristics, offers an entry to the political in accordance with the conditions and possibilities of the subjects who inhabit the school. At this level, Priestley and Xenofontos (2021, p. 5) state that teachers are the ones who give meaning to the curriculum, highlighting their important role as translators in curriculum policy processes. In this regard, they argue that the curriculum as a social practice leads to consider the role of teachers as curriculum-makers and wonder how their professional agency could be developed to make this happen. Perceiving translation as a micropolitical practice, the teacher becomes the translator and the author of the curriculum.

The school is the intermediate policy space between the curricular proposals that pretend to be universal, such as supra, macro and meso, and the exquisite particularity of each didactic triangle, recognized at the nano level. Given the premise that universality cannot be preserved without being translated, micropolitics does not resist universal proposals and allows itself to be subjected to some translation. But a school will not succeed in translating, via deconstruction, curricular policies without the recognition of hegemony, present in politics. Just as translation is an impossible task, because it never exhausts the production of meaning of the betrayed text, no political task that involves making one decision among many can be put into practice without the recognition of hegemony. On the other hand, for the elaboration of a micropolitical synthesis, there is a risk of confusing consensus with the agreements considered in the school. The combination of hegemony and the achievement of consensus cancels out any differences arising from the particularities of a translation. Because a decision that claims to be hegemonic and consensual is nothing more than a premise that legitimizes the majority, discarding difference. It is worth remembering that when teachers construct the meaning of the school curriculum, they confirm themselves as subjects who turn translation into a curricular policy practice. Therefore, if the deconstruction of curricular policies is in itself a task of "politics," it is imperative to recognize hegemony as that tendency of power that puts at risk any particularity, difference and minority. In this way, micropolitics seeks the achievement of contingent and precarious agreements that confirm the handcrafted and practical assembly of school life.

The meaning of secondary education

As a macro-political communication device, the curriculum is a discourse intended to communicate ideas about school-based education. Being one discourse among many, it is elaborated by highlighting key concepts, the ways in which they give meaning to the text and the devices chosen for the text to circulate among teachers who become readers, translators and authors of the curriculum.

Without intending to carry out an exhaustive analysis of the curriculum documents, I am interested in demonstrating, through transversal readings, the curriculum policies for secondary education in Argentina, Brazil, Chile and Mexico. Focusing on the education of young people, the Latin American academia made contributions and suggestions about the national curricular documents. With political frequencies that combine the crisis in secondary education with changes in government, these macro-political documents have points in common. Argentina and Brazil emphasize "school trajectories" with their "pedagogical itineraries," the former, and "life projects" and their "formative itineraries," the latter. In Chile, policies focus on comprehensive education, combined with the organization of school knowledge by disciplines. In Mexico, in 2022, a reform of basic education is designed, which includes secondary education, and considers interculturality as an "integrating axis" where the curriculum is contextualized and designed in the school.

Choosing concepts that nucleate the organization of the curriculum is a discursive decision that accompanies the process of translation and deconstruction, putting conceptual stability at risk. As Derrida argues when he states that there are changes from one context to another, it could happen that "life project" (for example) carries another signifier or that the school gives it another meaning, different from that of the document that presents it. In each rewriting of the "life project," teachers as readers, translators and authors may betray macro policies by creating new meanings for the education of young people. It is this translation that demonstrates that the meanings of the curricular text, far from being transcendental, as if they were sealed in the document, are extremely circumstantial.

Argentine, Brazilian, Chilean and Mexican policies share the idea of the right to education as an inalienable attribute for children and young people and the education laws of each of these countries uphold it as a key legal principle. Following Mouffe's (2012) theory of democracy, I argue that, in the current Latin American context, the democratic principle of the power of the people re-emerges, although, this time configured by the liberal discourse that gives value to individual freedoms and human rights. I wonder what is the meaning of the right to education in these countries. It may be understood as the right to learn, the right to stay in school, the right to preserve the working conditions of teachers, the right not to have their status as students undermined, etc., but I find some caveats in it. The tandem between rights and freedom puts under suspicion the wide range of inclusion that implies thinking in terms of human rights. Despite the fact that the right to education is enshrined in law, the curricular policies developed for this purpose do not seem to be sufficient to guarantee that young Argentines, Brazilians, Chileans and Mexicans have access to school education. Remaining in school can become a cliché that naturalizes the curriculum as a pedagogical text and reassures the States, as they guarantee this right. Staying in school does not mean learning, learning does not mean being educated and being educated may not be the same as becoming a student. Moreover, "permanence" in school creates its antonyms such as dropout and desertion. The latter, in turn, enables school failure, as a concept created to highlight the maladjustment of a student to school, but which could also mean the indifference of the school to the right to education and the scarcity of translations of curricular policies. In the contingency for the choice of concepts through which the curriculum is expressed, the right was cheated by failure. This scourge refers to the institutional lack of stability to sustain macro policies in secondary education and the fragility of the school curriculum that evidences universality, rather than particularity and difference. But above all, it shows the exclusion with which the school plays as one more institution of the social gear that marks cultural, racial and gender segregation. In the enclosure of a circular process, which turns without being resolved, the right to education in Latin American secondary schools forces the school to include young people excluded from the educational system.

School trajectories and life plan

When Argentina and Brazil choose concepts such as "school trajectories" and "life project" they awaken the reader's imagination toward biographical, subjective, self-reflective processes that make visible the student and his or her formation process within the school. However, once again the deception of circumstance raises suspicions about the place of the subject in these policies, questioning the relationship between meanings and signifiers. Since 2009, Argentine secondary education understands trajectories as "the path through which equivalent learning is acquired from a common set of knowledge" (Resolution CFE N°84/09, p. 5). Mentioning the pathway for the acquisition of learning of common knowledge demonstrates curricular policies designed for students whose subjectivity is suppressed by denying it in the recognition of equivalent learning of common knowledge. On the other hand, school trajectories describe different states, referring to themselves as necessary, real, interrupted, successful or discontinuous, and explain the assimilation of the trajectory to a path that places the emphasis on the development of learning rather than on the subject affected by his or her training process. However, betraying the meaning of the Argentine text, it is tempting to move from the learning process to the trajectory in order to identify it with the biography - from school and extracurricular - as the path taken to become a student. On the other hand, the notion of school trajectory of the Federal Council of Education (CFE) does not compromise the systemic organization of educational administration. As the structuring of secondary education remains intact and unchallenged, the right to education begins to be threatened.

As a nodal concept for Argentine secondary education, I wonder if trajectory were a metaphor, what would it replace?, what does it mean that the Argentine curriculum recognizes school trajectories?, with what other signifier could the meaning of trajectory be referred to? On the other hand, according to how it is stated in the national documents, I keep asking, who is the addressee of school trajectories: the teachers, the school curriculum or the student?

Meanwhile, the 2018 curriculum for secondary education in Brazil presents the concept "life project." This is how it is presented by The Common National Curriculum Base (BNCC, *Base Nacional Común Curricular*):

> In this way, the life project is what students seek, project and redefine throughout their trajectory, a construction that accompanies the development of identity(ies), in contexts traversed by a culture and social demands that are articulated, sometimes to promote, sometimes to limit their desires.
>
> (BNCC, pp. 472–473)

It manifests the articulation with the so-called Fundamental Education (Primary Education) and it considers the student's life. It attends to their integral formation, personal and social development. According to the document, this construction of young people's lives can take place inside and outside the school. The role of the latter is to assist the student who is immersed in a culture. Brazilian academia has made criticisms of the life project (Macedo and Miller, 2022; Barros and Días, 2023; Belleza, 2023) considering that it is a proposal that responds to liberal political ideals, a product of antagonistic struggles for the hegemony of the State in the curriculum. They argue that it fosters values such as entrepreneurship, innovation, cooperation, adaptation, autonomy and claims the student to be the protagonist of his or her own schooling process, as a process that is achieved through success. Far from proposing collective activities, it focuses on the individual experience of each student. According to Barros and Días (2023) its enunciation leaves no room for contingency, always seeking indispensable conditions of necessity and the idea of a foreseeable future. According to the BNCC the life project requires from the student self-knowledge and self-care (p. 495), freedom, autonomy, critical awareness and responsibility (p. 570) and is in accordance with the ideals of justice, ethics and citizenship (p. 471). Once again, it could be exposed to the deception and betrayal of the text to play with other meanings of this signifier that exposes magic in individual life processes as a curricular policy.

In 2022, Mexico develops a curriculum reform for Basic Education that includes Preschool, Primary and Secondary Education. Radically changing the tone of previous proposals, this one is positioned in a deliberative curriculum betting on the "Analytical Program of the school," that is, the translation of the curricular proposal from the particular conditions of the school and the neighborhood where it is located. To this end, it creates the concept of "co-design," which focuses on the role of the teacher as the author and designer of the curriculum, being able to incorporate contents that are not part of the so-called "synthetic design" (the national document). According to the 2022 Curriculum "this training-appropriation process will be permanent, since it is assumed that the contextualization of the contents to meet the regional, local, contextual and situational characteristics of the teaching and learning process is in charge of the teachers" (*Plan de Estudio de Educación Preescolar, Primaria y Secundaria 2022*, pp. 11–12).

It introduces pending topics in the curricula of the region, such as interculturality and racial and gender debates. Regarding the presentation of the contents, they are organized in four broad and interdisciplinary formative fields: (1) Languages; (2) Knowledge and scientific thought; (3) Ethics, nature and societies; and (4) Human and community. On these fields, the teacher, as author, attends to contextualization and co-design. In addition, this curricular reform offers textbooks called "Free Textbooks" (LTG, *Libros de texto gratuitos*), which are distributed by the Secretary of Public Education (SEP, *Secretaría de Educación Pública*). These are elaborated on the basis of the knowledge present in the fields and of the learning development processes in force in the synthetic programs. The LTGs generated a lot of criticism among academics and public opinion for considering them part of an indoctrinating reform. Another interesting aspect is the view of assessment as part of the curricular process and not as something separate and apart from the tasks of the school curriculum, which accompanies basic education, with the autonomy of the teacher's work. Regarding the latter, it is argued that,

> The professional autonomy of teachers is recognized in order to contextualize the contents of the study programs according to the social, territorial, cultural and educational reality of the students, as well as the criteria for the evaluation of learning, the didactics of their discipline, interdisciplinary collegiate work, and their teacher training.
>
> (*Plan de Estudio de Educación Preescolar, Primaria y Secundaria 2022*, p. 68)

Without as much centrality as the "life project" of Brazil's curriculum or the "school trajectories" of Argentina's, Mexico's design mentions a "personal project" as the interaction between each student's learning and the content offered by the teacher.

Although organized by disciplines, Chile's "Curricular Bases for Secondary Education" of 2015, mentions, like Brazil, comprehensive education. This includes "spiritual, ethical, moral, affective, intellectual, artistic and physical dimensions, through the transmission and cultivation of values, knowledge and skills" (*Bases Curriculares 7° básico a 2° medio*, p. 16). Responding to liberal democratic principles, it upholds freedom of education and the right to education as core concepts. Almost in line with Brazil's design, it encourages students to elaborate "the first definitions" of a life project that allows them to assume commitments and responsibilities (*Bases Curriculares 7° básico a 2° medio*, p. 20).

"The common" in the Latin American curriculum

In these four countries, the curricular documents considered "foundations" for secondary education are elaborated in accordance with what is stated in the respective education regulations. The relationship between regulations and foundations is the first mark that distinguishes education policies from curriculum policies. The latter tend to be invisible, with the understanding that any decision of this type is considered as an educational policy, thus taking away the specificity of action from the curriculum. I mentioned earlier that, in the curricular policies of these countries, there is a common thread that links the right to education (for students), autonomy and freedom of teaching (for teachers). I have added in parentheses the addressees, which are understood in an almost naturalized way, although it could be interpreted the other way around, as the right to education for teachers and the autonomy and freedom for students.

Autonomy and freedom are presented as confusing values where the ideas of liberalism are mixed with good intentions for the American continent, didactic challenges and micropolitics. Without discarding a rare desire to make good results in the PISA tests coexist with the conditions of teaching and learning in each school class. Like all desires, there is a load of utopia that makes it impossible, but at the same time it proves to be elaborated by the mixture of common sense, consensus and hegemony that turn it into a universal statement. The tension between the global and the local makes the movement of curriculum policies possible, demonstrating its dynamics.

As a politically impossible task, Latin American curricular policies focus on "the common" pretending to achieve inclusion of all diversities (cultural, social, racial, gender, etc.). However, decided in the heat of hegemony, this concept only encourages exclusion. The definition of "the common" is the answer to the canonical political question of what knowledge is the most valuable and whose knowledge has the most valuable. Nothing is more impersonal than the common to all, nothing more misguided than the illusion of believing in the common as a condition for everyone to be represented in the curriculum. This is the most important problem afflicting Latin American curriculum policies. When it pretends to respond to the right to education by creating a condition of the common that does no more than confirm that there is knowledge more valuable than other and that the denomination of common presents a partiality granted by power relations. In the previous chapter, we saw how interculturality is a concept gained in the curriculum that breaks down the official school culture by trying to give value to all cultural expressions, whatever the groups. In other words, "the majority" would not apply as a criterion for defining common knowledge in a curriculum. With respect to interculturality, Gallardo Gutiérrez maintains that:

> Herein lies the conceptual tension that is constitutive for the construction of an intercultural curriculum, since it forces us to think of the notion of curriculum from the common, not from homogeneity. That is to say, if diversity forces us to think in the particular, in the local, the thesis on intercultural education for all forces us to think in the common, in the national, and the result of this exercise projects, then, a different position on the general and the particular.
>
> From the logic of articulation in Laclau (1993), the national would be the session of local identity in a constant tension for the representation of locals becoming nationals.
>
> (Gallardo Gutiérrez, 2015, p. 74)

If "the common" is a symbolic construction created to guarantee the right to education, it only turns the latter into an empty signifier, co-opted by hegemony, which universally decides a single meaning of access and permanence of children and youngsters in school. But what is hidden with the fulfillment of the right to education, instituting the common, is that the notion of "included subject" will have been defined on the basis of a social and cultural prototype of student. In a scheme of agonistic politics (Mouffe, 2014) I warn that the right to education is a condition that enables democracy, but lacks the figure of the adversary. As if the common, as a condition for guaranteeing rights, were defined without tensions, interests or negotiations. Assuming that the common is constructed by consensus configures it outside of democracy. What generates tension around this condition is the way in which curricular policies are designed to fulfill the right to education. Far from this, Mouffe (2012) defines difference and pluralism as conditions for being. The author argues that democracy contains the paradox of being defined between the liberal proclamation of human rights and popular sovereignty in the democratic imaginary, and adds that in a liberal democracy it is legitimate to establish limits to popular sovereignty in the name of freedom, hence, for this author, democracy is paradoxical (Mouffe, 2012). So, when macro policies are organized on the basis of the commons as an alleged guarantee of rights, I wonder what is non-negotiable in that which the curriculum defined as common.

Curricular policies for compulsory education are a problem that should be included among the problems of life in democracy. Far from attributing a single option to its subjects, democracy, closer to pluralism, implies "developing the capacity to see things from a multiplicity of perspectives" (Mouffe, 2014, p. 28). From this author's position, the notion of "the common" inscribed in curriculum documents is closer to consensus, which resists accepting a political construction. When curriculum policies highlight "the common" as a central problem in their enunciation, they omit to state the processes of tensions and negotiations through which it has been established. That is to say, how a certain content of the common is agreed upon, discarding others. In addition to their proximity to pluralism and conflict, curricular policies are articulated on the basis of the recognition of difference in contingency.

There remains a great challenge for Latin American curricula, or at least in the countries mentioned here, to allow compulsory education to include everyone without homogenizing the subjects that are included. Returning to what I stated above, it is in the translation made by teachers as authors of the curriculum in each school, where this discourse acquires materiality and meaning. But a tension is created between macro and micro politics, leaving the inclusion of all as a school decision, without the State being able to detect the local movements. Among the countries analyzed, Mexico, with its 2022 reform, is the one that changes the equation between the right to education and inclusion, stating that "for the New Mexican School, the common is understood as a principle of co-responsibility and co-participation among those members of the school community who are committed to the formation and emancipation of students" (*Plan de Estudios de la Educación Básica 2022*, p. 22). In short, in the relationship between macro and micro policies, the State should guarantee inclusion in all circumstances.

Note

1 Institutional governance is found in politics, while politics accounts for the democratic ideal of social construction.

4 The promise of post-*Bildung*

The concept of *Bildung* is assumed in a permanent tension between ambiguity and prestige. In spite of this, both academics and curriculum policy makers see *Bildung* as a concept of great importance for education because of its relationship with knowledge and the intellectual and moral development of the subject. Since its emergence in the late 18th century and coined by Wilhelm von Humboldt, *Bildung* has revolved around the relationship between education, society and culture and has the particularity of a double meaning. On the one hand, it represents the education of "oneself" and on the other hand, the education of "one in society." Within this framework, an important contribution to school-based education is the notion of "*Bildung-centered Didaktik*", also derived from the German tradition.

The historical persistence of *Bildung* allows it to reach, with its characteristic ambiguity and prestige, the present times, which are far from the modern scenarios of the 18th century. Moreover, trying to install this debate in the Latin America of the 21st century. To ask myself if *Bildung* makes sense in Latin America is a propitious question that enables me to study its meaning and its relationship with society and school in the unstable and convulsed present times. Returning to this concept allows me to rethink it on the basis of Post-Critical Theories, acquiring new meanings that go beyond the universality of a meta-narrative, as recognized by Modernity. Now, despite its Neo-Enlightenment history, it is undeniable the educational potential that the concept of *Bildung* contains, and how it broadens its meaning toward the relationship with didactics, more appropriately called *Didaktik*. To this day, *Bildung* remains a prominent idea in education to improve both the institutional understanding of schooling and the relationship between education, society and culture in the formation of the subject and its relationship with himself/herself and with others. The notion of formation that accompanies the constellations of Brazil and Mexico, in which expert academics influence others, is a pedagogical idea between those who possess knowledge and those who wish to possess it.

In the presentation given by Rebekka Horlacher at the "I European Conference on Curriculum Studies", at the University of Minho (Braga, Portugal) in

DOI: 10.4324/9781003475279-4

2013, entitled "Curriculum studies as an import from abroad – the case of Switzerland", she recovers what was expressed in the chapter she authored in the second edition of the *International Handbook of Curriculum Research* on curriculum in Switzerland (Horlacher and De Vicenti, 2014). In her presentation, she establishes relations between curriculum and didactics without leaving out the debate on *Bildung*. This perspective, equally considered by Westbury et al. (2015)[1] inspires me to include the topic in the organization of the "Área del Curriculum" (Curriculum Area), when I take over as full professor in 2015 at UNR. From then on *Bildung* is part as a topic of the seminar "Curriculum and Didactics: conceptual, historical and epistemological horizons" linked not only to *Bildung-centered Didaktik* but also to the relation curriculum and *didaktik* (Morelli, 2021c). The wisdom of incorporating this theme continues to be confirmed by the students' surprise when they discover the educational power of *Bildung*. With the analysis of the film *The Reader* (2008) directed by Stephen Daldry and starring Ralph Fiennes and Kate Winslet, they travel to a post-war Germany in which a young high school student and an adult, illiterate woman begin a love affair in which reading aloud literary classics and sex form a transaction. The stills, metaphors and dialogues shed enough content to understand through the language of cinema the relationship between society, education and culture nucleated in a concept such as *Bildung*. The ambiguity between this and the Second World War is part of the discussion: was it necessary to destroy the idea of *Bildung* to give rise to the horror of the Holocaust, or does the obsession for distinction go as far as genocide? The second genocide of the 20th century, after the Armenian genocide in 1915, "after all, who speaks today of the annihilation of the Armenians?" Hitler would have asked in 1939, shortly before invading Poland (Granovsky, 2014).

At the "6th Curriculum Studies Conference" at Melbourne University, I had presented a paper entitled "Curriculum and *Bildung* as a Teaching Language" which contained thoughts on the relationship between them and teaching, including also *didaktik*. Reviving the event of the Oslo Congress and the question about the difference between didactics and *didaktik* that Westbury asks Hopmann, I propose articulations between Curriculum Theory and Didaktik Tradition including in this relationship a discussion about *Bildung*. Talking with Jeong-Hee Kim, from Texas Tech University, with whom we were sharing the session, I express my concern about the wisdom of teaching *Bildung* in the third year of undergraduate education. Kim looks at me with wide eyes and replies "Wow, *Bildung* in the undergraduate program! When I teach it in the doctoral program, the students tell me: Why didn't we discover this concept earlier!". This anecdote helped me to support an early discovery of such a promising concept and I decided to continue teaching it in undergraduate education.

This enabled me to study it in a non-modern context, including Lyotard's (2004/1979) questioning of the project of modernity and the destruction of grand narratives. The research entitled "Rewriting *Bildung* in Postmodernity" accompanied from 2020 to 2023 channeling the problem in the suspension of a modern, Neo-Enlightenment and Central European *Bildung* to build little narratives of a powerful educational concept, with postcritical categories and in a Latin American context. Meanwhile, interested in this approach to be treated in postgraduate training, the director of the PhD in Education at UNR, Fernando Avendaño, invites me to present a seminar that I entitled "The concept of *Bildung*: between tradition and promise" in reference to the article by Lars Løvlie (2002) "The promise of *Bildung*", which appears in the Special Issue of the *Journal of Philosophy of Education*[2] edited by him and Paul Standish, which deals with the scope of the idea of *Bildung* after modernity, questioning its meaning today. This seminar was given dozens of times for cohorts of Argentine, Ecuadorian, Brazilian, Colombian, and Uruguayan students. As in undergraduate training, once again the intellect of the students was surprised to discover a concept, little dealt with in our academic culture. Discussions with doctoral students deepen with the reading of -at least-one *Bildungsroman* among those offered, *David Copperfield* (Dickens, 2014/1850); *The Catcher in the Rye* (Salinger, 2014/1945) and *Demian* (Hesse, 2018/1919). Modern formative novels, where their main characters are young bourgeois males and material needs are not a variable in their lives. Despite the macho and bourgeois characteristics of this literary genre, they are young men who live accompanied by the conflicting question about who they are and what they want to become.

The main characters of these novels contrasts with the young Latin American schoolchildren, those for whom the Brazilian curriculum proposes the "Life Project", the Argentine curriculum the "School Trajectories" and the new Mexican school, the "personal project." Furthermore, I believe that it would not be necessary to get to the school of 2024 to understand the difference between the main characters of the novels and the Latin American students. And although the school continues to preserve its modern traditions with a lot of resistance to change them, even so, we do not find them. I believe that what happens is that the school still does not stand the personal conflict and doubts of the student. The process of formation that *Bildung* conveys, which occupies, in my opinion, the years of youth that coincide with high school, needs time to deal with the conflict of knowing who one wants to be. This life of dubious morals and questioned identity is not tolerated by (secondary) school. The school cancels a slow, rocky process of formation that needs to be resolved by the relationship of the subject with himself or herself.

I admit the fascination that the concept of *Bildung* provokes in me when I think of formation associated with the relationship between curriculum and *didakitk*. I consider that they can be understood as a single field (Morelli, 2021c) sustained by complementary relationships, articulated by teaching. Reviving the debate on *Bildung*, at the risk of bringing to the present a modern concept from the German tradition, increases the possibilities of enhancing it. Unlike those who argue that this concept has no place in today's societies, I am interested in giving it the status of a floating signifier in order to elaborate a notion of post-*Bildung* that disseminates it in little Latin narratives. Breaking with the universality of the concept enables to think it in the difference of local, circumstantial and contingent practices. To this end, I consider two aspects for this conceptual reconstruction linked to the subject and the *Bildungsroman* as a literary genre that accompanies proposing metaphors for formation.

The subject

Postcritical theories distrust the idea of the subject because of the centrality it has taken in modernity. Revising it implies inscribing it in the relationship with the environment, multiculturalism, language, accepting that each case will be a small, minimal and particular narrative. These subjects emerge from silences and invisibility, manifesting themselves through feminisms, disabilities, sexual identities, blackness and anything that highlights difference. It is a subject that arrives at the pedagogical scene of formation with altered roles because it will be constituted by the relationship between those who have knowledge and those who have the desire for that knowledge, regardless of whether they are teachers or students. On the other hand, in American territory, it will be necessary to consider the "subject of conquest" as the one which is simultaneously the object of colonization and a foreigner.

A challenge presented by an idea of post-*Bildung* is to rethink the subject in the tension between the itself and theories such as that proposed by posthumanism, which includes not only human beings, but extends its consideration to other living beings. From here, I find the subject in an intermediate space between humanism, questioning the arrogance with which man has occupied the center of history, and posthumanism. In a new notion of subject and its relationship with society Braidotti (2015, p. 23) states that:

> We need to project new social, ethical and discursive schemes of subject formation in order to face the profound changes we are facing. This implies that we have to learn to think differently about ourselves. I assume the posthuman condition as an opportunity to encourage the search for alternative schemes of thought, knowledge and self-representation with respect to the dominant ones. The posthuman condition urgently calls us to reconsider, critically and creatively, who and what we are becoming in this process of metamorphosis.
>
> (Braidotti, 2015, p. 23)

There is a change in what is understood by subject and subjectivity. I consider it important not to forget about it, but also to provoke the necessary shift to include it in the post-scenarios. The training process or pedagogical scene, as I prefer to call it, has already decentered the teacher (Morelli, 2021b) establishing new relationships in the pedagogical asymmetry. It is worthwhile, then, to extend this concern in order to rethink subjectivity in the events of postmodern times. To do so, I turn to revive *Bildung* trying to deconstruct it as the grand modern narrative. To move it from the modern chest of German Neo-Enlightenment and to use its potential in the relationship between curriculum and *didaktik*. In my opinion, those who reject its treatment, precisely because its Neo-Enlightenment and modern characteristics, recognize it as an empty signifier, in Laclau's words, whose meaning, defined by hegemony, could never vary. On the contrary, I intend to take it to contexts that set-in motion the language games (Wittgenstein, 2021/1953) that allow it, transitorily, to have more than one meaning and that, at the same time, this depends on an agreement between speakers. Its inscription in the "internationalization" of curriculum studies will make its borders translucent, leaving the context of origin behind in order to be thought for other subjects in other societies.

Rescuing the ambiguity of the concept of *Bildung*, it is not only the relationship of the subject with society that deserves to be analyzed, but, above all, the relationship of the subjects with themselves, with their inwardness and with what they wish to be. I return to the nodal questions of the formation process, contained in *Bildung* and continued in post-*Bildung*: Who am I and what do I want to become (Fabre, 2011), who am I as a (Latin) American and what do I want to become in order to continue being (Latin) American? To the canonical question, as didactic as it is political, regarding whose knowledge has more value, is added another more personal, interior, subjective question with which the subject continues to grapple with itself in the thick journey of their formation. The construction of the *self* is installed in times in which the principle of reality has been abandoned, in Freud's categories (1981/1911), exacerbating the principle of pleasure and hedonism. Times of selfies with which the subject presents himself in society, changing their own image, fabricating another one that deceives the viewer of the image. This distortion is part of the subject that pretends to be self-determined in the eyes of others.

In a post-*Bildung* debate it is essential to refer to self-determination as that obligatory passage of the *self*. Klafki (2015, p. 87) mentions self-determination as a denomination in the classic texts on the subject arguing that it is presented as a synonym for "freedom, emancipation, autonomy, responsibility, reason and independence." All terms that value the distinguished formation of the subject who has become a citizen. He also states that "*Bildung* was understood as a qualification for reasonable self-determination." Without wishing to reinstate these modern terms, I do consider that it is worth recovering self-determination and doing something with it. Klafki (1998, pp. 313–314) recovers three moments of *Bildung* in its relation to his *Critical-Constructive*

Didaktik. These are composed of self-determination, co-determination and solidarity. In the author's own words:

- Self-determination: Each and every member of society is to be enabled to make independent, responsible decisions about her or his individual relationships and interpretations of an interpersonal, vocational, ethical or religious nature.
- Co-determination: Each and every member of society has the right but also the responsibility to contribute together with others to the cultural, economic, social and political development of the community.
- Solidarity: As I understand the term, it means that the individual right to self-determination and possibilities for co-determination can only be represented and justified if it is associated not only with the recognition of equal rights but also with active help those opportunities for self-determination and co-determination are limited or non-existent due social conditions, lack of privilege, political restrictions, or oppression.

Klafki (1998, p. 314)

It is interesting to recover these three moments for the achievement of (self-) formation in which subjective, particular instances are articulated with social instances where, from my point of view, solidarity surpasses rights. Articulating self-determination with instances of co-determination brings the debate to life in society and the cooperation of those who inhabit it. It justifies that it would not make sense if we were a group of self-determined subjects without knowing what to do in the society we inhabit. Co-determination strengthens social bonds and if we transfer this social scheme to the school class, it is enhanced in pedagogical tasks (according to the critical-constructive didactics proposed by the author). But the scheme proposed by Klafki is completed only with the third moment, which is solidarity. Solidarity makes possible the achievement of any of the other two moments of formation. It is the bond of solidarity that brings the subject closer to self-determination and co-determination. Solidarity as a value that differs from justice, in didactic terms. More than with the equality of rights, as understood by the author, I see in solidarity the possibility of recognizing the difference and working in solidarity based on it.

In 2013, the Ministry of Education of the province of Santa Fe in Argentina launched the "Vuelvo a estudiar" (I'm going back to school) program for young people who had dropped out of high school to return to school at any time of the year. As you know, the school year in Argentina runs from March to December. In the month of June, students were still arriving in the classrooms. Talking to a principal of these schools, she expressed her annoyance at having to receive "dropouts from the educational system" out of term and argued that it was unfair that these students shared the classroom with others who had started the academic year in March. Regarding her annoyance,

I replied to the principal that it was not a problem of justice but of solidarity. That one day we are helping young people to go back to school, and that in the future we do not know which group we will have to be in solidarity with to help them solve which problem. In the year 2020, the isolation due to the Covid-19 pandemic showed that the problems in school change radically. Then, I remembered this principal and her request for justice to order the school scene and my proposal of solidarity. I thought, in 2013 we had to be in solidarity with young people who could not get to school for various reasons: teenage pregnancy, leaving home, hospitalization. During the virtual pandemic education, I symbolically remembered each of these young people and thought that, had they attended high school in 2020, their problems would not have been such. Instead, the problem to be addressed through solidarity was how to bring the new materiality proposed by digital languages and virtuality to young people who, without problems such as pregnancy, hospitalization or dropping out of home, needed connectivity in order not to become a "school dropout."

The concept of *Bildung* shares the conceptual ambiguity of curriculum and didactics/*didaktik*. Engaging it with Wittgenstein's language games and Laclau's floating signifiers implies constructing its notion according to the subjects and their circumstance. That at present there are at least three ways of understanding the continuity of *Bildung* means that it is far from having a single meaning applicable to all situations of formation. The constitutive difference of the subject is marking it and the diversity of circumstances, too. It is therefore possible that there is a continuity, from its critical perspective, of the notion proposed by von Humboldt that aims at the emancipation of a subject by means of autonomy. At the same time, supra-national organizations justify standardized evaluations such as those proposed by PISA in the name of complex capacities acquired through *Bildung*. But also that in the 21st century reflections on *Bildung* and postmodernity have begun. This shows that we are facing a concept that uses its potential even to define itself. I agree with Biesta (2002) when he refers to it as a complex concept and I share the question about how general it can be, disengaging from a concept of universal formation. Likewise, I share with Horlacher (2016) that this is a fuzzy concept, of unstable demarcation in which the relationship between inner and outer formation can be considered.

Post-*Bildung* in art-induced reflection

The first thing that strikes me about the movie *The Reader* is the time game: the film begins with an adult Michael Berg in 1995. When he was 15 years old, meets Hanna Schmitz, 35 years old, in the year 1958. Eight years later, in 1964, when Michael is a law student, the trial for the 1944 arson in a church inside an SS extermination camp takes place, Hanna is one of the defendants. In 1988 Hanna, serving a life sentence, is released (although she decides not to do so) and on a date, probably 1998, Michael travels to New York to fulfill the assignment left by Hanna.

The first images share the neatness and mess on the countertop of Michael's apartment in Berlin, 1995. An adult Michael prepares breakfast for himself and the woman who has been visiting him since the night before. The mess, through the dirty dishes buried in the sink, foreshadows the continuing scenes of violence, dubious morals, and what Adorno (1969) himself calls the "population explosion" as a metaphor for the humanitarian crisis of the 20th century. The disorder continues in the scene that follows, when alone, standing under the frame of his bedroom door, he silently contemplates, without entering, the mess left on the bed after a night as a couple. A train passing in front of his window takes him to the past, where he finds himself at the age of 15.

Hanna, 35 years old and illiterate, asks to be read aloud. She demands to be read to as if she were a child, while her inner adult asks her to hide her condition. Rude, harsh, obedient, unworthy, she accepts what her life has in store without proposing that her desire should change anything. She ignores the possibility of intervening in her own life. She represents the destruction of *Bildung*, necessary to annihilate the different. Two doubts hover over the film, leaving the viewer with an ambivalent feeling, leaving them to wonder about the sensitivity and vulnerability of the female protagonist.

Her self-determination alters the scene. She learns to read with the solidarity of Michael who sends her taped novels and of the prison library that lends her books. Deciphering Anton Chekhov's novel *Lady with the dog*, she becomes human and no longer feels like an animal. Her late self-determination shows her own life, in denied and blurred letters that become clear when she reads alone. Her self-determination allows her to choose her death. Barefoot and elevated on a pile of books, she finds suicide in the letters that were denied to her throughout her life and, once deciphered, she leads herself to liberation.

For a long time I was looking for a *Bildungsroman* where the protagonist was a woman dealing with contemporary issues tinged by her gender and whose social status posed disadvantages regarding education. I am probably not making mention of a formative novel, or perhaps I should be referring to the rewriting of the genre. This happens with *Furia: a novel* by Saied Méndez (2023). Its protagonist is Camila Beatriz Hassan, a young woman who lives in the city of Rosario, a very good soccer player, a sport to which she wants to dedicate herself professionally once she finishes high school. The economic vicissitudes of this young girl force her to use an old and cheap cell phone, limited in technology (because the one she had was stolen at the corner of her house), to play soccer with broken boots, to look for a job to pay for the South American tournament at the end of the year. Camila lives at home, a small apartment with her parents and her brother Pablo, who plays soccer as a striker in the first division of Rosario Central, is very talented, but unwilling to train. As in many Argentine families that have boys dedicated to professional soccer, Pablo is the family's hope for economic improvement. Camila hides from her parents that she trains during the week and plays soccer on weekends. Faced with different circumstances, Camila lies, deceives and hides. Her father Andrés, a violent macho man, controls the family at will and her mother Isabel is a docile dressmaker who works from home and whose own life was put off by her children and husband.

Like many young Argentinean women, Camila is committed to social issues such as the legalization of abortion and actively participates in every protest claiming for the "appearance alive" of teenage girls who frequently disappear and swell the list of femicides. After school, she teaches English to children who need support, as well as food and some clothes, at the "Buen Pastor", an institution of the Catholic Church.

Although her father had sentenced her to be a lesbian because of her passion for soccer, Camila fights for women soccer players not to be stereotyped. Episodes of gender-based violence, such as the murder of a young woman, sister of a friend, and a beating by her father, tinge her path to self-determination. Her decision to finish high school, to refuse her boyfriend's offer to take her home to live with him in Milan and to decide not to study medicine in order to devote herself to soccer mark the end of her long process of formation as a subject of *Bildung*.

The difference between Wilhem Meister, David Copperfield, Emil Sincler, Holden Caulfield are found within this argumentation of Horlacher (2016, pp. 15–16) when she says that in German novels, such as the case of *Wilhem Meister's Apprenticeship*, the protagonists are boys from bourgeois and wealthy families, while American and English novels also include girl/woman protagonists whose families belong to the working class who break free from their stories through talent, skill, fate or luck. Still, there remain differences between these characters and Camila Hassan, who finds herself in an era of great perished narratives, where the protagonist does not question herself in the key of modern rationality (although in the case of Holden Caulfield some of this is already noticeable). Camila is a young woman living in a Latin American city, whose subjectivity, individual and private, does not cease to be affected by the conditions of life, great economic difficulties, surrounded by others with similar difficulties. Social, material and feminine vulnerability accompany her on the path that leads her to what she wants to become.

After addressing a post-*Bildung* centered on the absences that the concept has had up to now, installing it in a Neo-Enlightenment era, I would like to retrieve the curricular policies for secondary education discussed in the previous chapter. With the best of intentions, the "Life Project" (Brazil), "School Trajectories" (Argentina) and "Personal Project" (Mexico) try to install a process that accompanies young people in their formation beyond school. All the criticisms that inscribe these projects in neo-liberal texts, that pretend with pragmatism to solve problems of young people's lives, absence of theoretical arguments that cooperate with their treatment in schools, etc., are valid. I propose to deconstruct the universality of these categories that make the curricula of secondary education to hang together. That the school can recognize the concept of *Bildung*, even if it has a wider scope and can recognize in it the formation of the subject, knowing that young people reflect beyond the school. This shift toward the subject of difference is part of the changes affecting the curriculum in Latin America. Thinking the subject of *Bildung* from within the Latin American school allows me to recover a process of formation that takes place between school and society, between oneself and others. In this way, solidarity is the means to relate in each (particular) case, *Bildung* and curriculum.

Notes

1 I consider this is a text that closes a trilogy composed by Hopmann, S. and Riquartz, K. (Eds.) (1995). *Didaktik and/or Curriculum*. Kiel: Institut für die Pädagogik der Naturwissenchaften an der Universität Kiel and Hopmann, S. and Gundem, B. (Eds.) (1998). *Didaktik and/or Curriculum: An International Dialogue*. New York: Perter Lang.

2 See *Journal of Philosophy of Education*, Vol. 36, No. 3, 2002.

5 Why not America?

The afternoon before the start of the "IX congreso de COMIE" (IX COMIE Congress) in the Mexican city of Merida I decided to spend a few hours at Progreso Beach. The seashore was empty, and the access was forbidden. When, after insistently requesting it, I finally managed to be the only person to be allowed to access the coast, I asked the waiter who came to serve, –could you tell me why I was not allowed earlier to access this place?–; –it is because the cruise is coming–, he answered me. –Cruise, what cruise?–, I asked, hoping that the word "cruise" meant something different from what I had understood. –The cruise–, he answered. –The ship with the Americans–. –So, if this place is reserved for Americans, it is for me, I am an American,– I told him. And I added to the young Mexican waiter: –You are also American.–

Why do we use America to refer to the United States and call the rest of the continent Latin America, or Ibero-America? Where is Canada in this distribution? It is true that, given the extension of the continent, the second largest after Asia, it is necessary to divide it in North and South, (where Central America is part of the North), a differentiation that is also symptomatic. But it is also true that the difference between North, Central and South America is more a colonial than a cartographic denomination: why not call it simply America? when did we stop calling it simply America? why is it common to identify America with the United States, and its inhabitants are called Americans? America, that continent created from a conquest, born on the threshold of modernity. A land of ancestors annihilated by force of armies, of a past without history, of stories without protagonists. A land where immigrants came seeking to calm famines, to escape wars, to improve the future of their children. Any American survivor is a descendant of a foreigner. Any survivor of the wrongly called "pre-Columbian America" is still trying to collect the pieces of identity taken away. Like a circular passage, the history of subjectivity always passes through the same places, honoring the folds of discourse. Then, the conquest is revived in migratory waves and identity is internally snatched. Why does the United States keep the signifier? Isn't the United States becoming more and more Latino? What is the meaning of being American? How has this meaning changed throughout the brief and modern American history?

DOI: 10.4324/9781003475279-5

We cannot understand the processes in the field of curriculum without evoking the hegemony of the United States over the rest of America. The consolidation of curriculum theory through technical theory institutes a notion of pragmatic curriculum that prevails in the rest of the continent for a good part of the 20th century. Its late start in the 1960s denotes that when Latin America enters the field of curriculum inheriting the *Curriculum Development* movement, it was just when the United States abandons it and begins to study its *Reconceptualization*, as Pinar (2013) calls it. Regarding the change between these two curricular paradigms, the author says:

> In general terms this describes the situation in U.S. curriculum studies after the national school reform of the 1960s. No longer were there conditions in place to support the institutional curriculum development Tyler's principles had organized. It was not only this scheme – which links outcomes to objectives, recasting teaching as implementation – that was to blame for the loss of professional agency, setting the stage for four decades of "school reform." It was this cataclysmic shift in the once close relationship between university-based professors and the public schools that forced the 1970s reconceptualization of curriculum studies in the United States.
>
> (Pinar, 2013, p. 8)

The adherence that Latin America has had with the technical perspective of the curriculum is supported by the hegemony exercised by the United States over the rest of the continent to which the US exports a model whose theory and practices were questioned. The dissemination in Latin America of a late *Tyler Rationale* marks an antagonism between it and the *Reconceptualization* movement which the US was already immersed into. This antagonism highlights a power scheme that differentiates the country that decides on the theories from the countries that receive the theories, between those who produce knowledge on curriculum and those who reproduce it. Latin America enters curriculum studies through technicality. With great difficulty, by the mid-1980s, it began to recognize practical perspectives that rethink teaching, the role of teachers and school life, and critical perspectives that recognize the social function of schools and the curriculum as a political construction. The shift from a curriculum by objectives to reconceptualization was a path that implied questioning 20 years of stagnant practices, subjected to military dictatorships in the countries of the continent. As a disjointed map, on the one hand, there were the practical perspectives derived from the University of Chicago, proposed by Schwab (1969) and Jackson (1991/1968). In the United Kingdom, strikingly, the proposal of Stenhouse (1975), which considered the curriculum as an "attempt" and a hypothesis to be implemented under certain conditions in practice, had more impact. Simultaneously, a Marxist perspective brought by Apple (1986, 1987, 2002), Giroux (1988) and Popkewitz (1994) contributed with perspectives for a curriculum of resistance and criticism, whose first educational ideas had been proposed in the continent by Paulo Freire from Brazil to all Latin America in the 1960s.

The entry of Latin America into the curriculum, recognized as an intellectual field, presents three events that inscribe it between colonization and emancipation. An event is a social symptom that denounces that something is happening. But it is subjectivity that recognizes it, because it becomes an event when what was previously tolerated is no longer tolerated. For Lazzarato (2006) an event has the form of a question and implies a problem rather than its solution. Hoping that another world is possible, it is always presented as a possibility, setting a new horizon. The author states that "only an event creates the possibility of a new object and the possibility of a new subject" (Lazzarato, 2006, p. 52). In a relationship between the material and the spiritual, he adds that "the world is not made of objects and subjects, but of a fabric of relations (physical, vital, social) that combine according to hierarchies constituted by the capture of a myriad of other individuals (physical, vital or human monads)" (Lazzarato, 2006, p. 57). According to Laclau and Mouffe (2010) an event can be identified as a moment in a temporal succession. The degree of contingency of an event allows its subjects to put under suspicion the relevance of the moment, granting different meanings to the event.

The first event in Latin American curricular studies is the translation into Spanish and distribution of works inscribed in the *Curriculum Development* movement. This task was carried out as part of the actions of the *Alliance for Progress* that took place between 1961 and 1970. This project considered one of the most important US aids to Latin America, consisted of granting 20 billion dollars to support democratic governments by improving homes, work and land, health, and schools. Paradoxically, given the pragmatic perspective to which the translated works belonged, they were used by the education policies of the *de facto* governments, which took place from the 1970s to the mid-1980s throughout Latin America's soil, except for Mexico (see Díaz Barriga, 2011; Kumar, 2011a; Morelli, 2016). Thus, the curriculum is associated with an idea of control, typical of dictatorial contexts and authoritarianism as the antagonistic opposite of democracy. It is also associated with a written document (teacher planning or syllabus), with the imperative of complying with what is prescribed regardless of what happens in practice. As a written document, it aims to control school life and the work of the teacher, dedicated to the correct implementation of what is stated in the document. In a neo-technicality, the second event is the standardization of curricular discourses (Morelli, 2010) that took place through the educational reforms imposed by multilateral credit agencies such as the World Bank and the Inter-American Development Bank in the 1990s. This period of reforms institutes what I call "curricular discourses" referring to those that involve the curriculum as a central aspect for change and innovation. It is a very productive decade for the curriculum, allowing even academics from outside the field to write about it. As is already known, these reforms proposed competency-based curricular models, curricular flexibility and installed standardized assessments both at the supra-level, such as PISA, and at the macro-political level in each of the nation states. The decade was tinged with educational reforms that globalization ensured were different for different sectors of the world. Thus, the curriculum in Latin America and the Caribbean, with its developing countries, is uniformly subjected to neoliberal educational policies that promulgated the privatization of education. It should be noted that, in the sectorization of globalization, Latin America is grouped together with Africa and Asia (although the latter two are also subdivided within the region). Educational reforms construct a notion of curriculum as a technological device that directs educational improvement toward social and economic growth. As a neo-technicist event, it reissues evaluation as educational accreditation and elaborates a taxonomy of contents that organize educational competencies.

As a breath of fresh air and deconstructing the proposals that demand control by government agencies far removed from the circumstances of each territory, the internationalization of the curriculum was instituted in the early 2000s. The creation of the International Association for the Advancement of Curriculum Studies and the Pinar keynote speech on the Internationalization of Curriculum Studies (see Chapter 2) in 2003 in Mexico, triggered this event. Also, the edition of the *International Handbook of Curriculum Research*, coordinated by Pinar (2003a), where many Latin American countries participate, becoming visible in curriculum studies. This situation is strengthened with the second edition of the *International Handbook of Curriculum Research* (Pinar, 2014a), in which more Latin American countries join the public debate. As an event, the internationalization of curriculum studies offers permeability to epistemological and cultural frontiers, confirming academic dialogues and conversations around the ways in which the curriculum is understood in each country, region or academic group. It poses a disruptive break with the two previous developments that caused the curriculum to be stagnated in the technical and efficiency-based reproduction that gave it a late start as an intellectual field in the region. In my opinion, it is an inflection of the movement of reconceptualization of the curriculum, which empowers it toward the commonwealth, giving it solvency throughout the world. With this, internationalization ends the instance that had moved the curriculum from pragmatic tasks, also recognized as a "crisis" (Pinar et al., 2008), to a reconceptualization that presents it as a phenomenological, teleological and political text. Moreover, the concept of "internationalization" is contrasted with that of "globalization" (as discussed in Chapter 2), exchanging the competitiveness and productivity of globalization, so harmful to this part of the world, for the solidarity and hospitality of international links as evidenced in the International Association for the Advancement of Curriculum Studies, or in other national or regional non-Latin American associations. Far from segregating, they accommodate academics from different territories, and this is how Latin American curriculum academics participate in congresses organized by Euro-ACS, AAACS, ACSA, in the edition of Transnational

Curriculum Inquiry (TCI) or in webinars or trainings throughout the world. Finally, in epistemological terms, internationalization enables dialogue between countries/regions by promoting the exchange of curriculum notions, theoretical approaches, research programs, national curriculum designs, etc. As the field of curriculum in Latin America consolidates through internationalization, it breaks with the chains that tied it to authoritarianism, first, and to neoliberal mercantilism, later, to inscribe itself in the language of hybridity, multiculturalism and the narration of its circumstances and histories that will lead it toward postcritical perspectives.

As in a soccer game of the curriculum with itself, it leads two to one. Two events in which the curriculum is exposed to the technical paradigm, where curriculum management is designed from universal levels such as the Alliance for Progress, the World Bank, and the Inter-American Development Bank, pretending that their policies improve implementation in schools. The first two events inscribe the field of curriculum publicly in pragmatism with a notion of curriculum linked exclusively to the syllabus. This offers Latin America a late task with respect to its inscription in curriculum studies and the oscillation between pragmatism, at one extreme, and phenomenology and critical sciences, at the other. Thus this field is built with the resistance that generates the tension between control and difference. It is internationalization, as an event, what promotes the change in the notion of curriculum, articulating paradigms that make the curriculum to be involved with social circumstances. But, above all, this third event allows the continent exchanges between regions and countries in a way that initiates complicated conversations (Pinar, 2012, 2014a) with similarities and differences, allowing transnational challenges. Thus, Latin American researchers can critique the course toward which the curricular field is moving (Pinar, 2014a). In a double sense, the internationalization of the curriculum expands the theoretical and geographic frontiers of the field (Pinar, 2014a). Thus, Latin American researchers can critique the course toward which the curriculum field is moving (Pinar, 2014a). In a double sense, the internationalization of the curriculum expands the theoretical and geographical boundaries of the field in Latin America, and simultaneously, links it to the world, making it visible.

Influenced by the movement of internationalization of the curriculum, when in 2015 I became a professor in the "Curriculum Area" in the bachelor's degree in education sciences at the UNR, I decided to incorporate a seminar entitled "Curriculum and Didactics: conceptual, historical and epistemological horizons", which I mentioned in the previous chapter about the concept of *Bildung*. This course, which has an annual duration, is organized as a journey through curriculum theory with the purpose of ending in the postcritical approaches of the present. After an introduction that establishes the importance of studying curriculum theory, the seminar continues with Franklin Bobbitt's efficiency in 1918 and his dispute with Dewey's progressivism, Ralph Tyler's hegemony, the launching of Sputnik in 1957 and the discipline-based curriculum reform where the Woods Hole Congress of 1959, a Bruner passionate about the structure of the disciplines and an early Schwab dedicated to the teaching of Biology are studied. The break in curriculum theory was proposed by a "second Schwab" who became a curriculum theorist, changing his direction toward practice in 1969, and from then on, the crossing of borders that placed the field of curriculum in the United Kingdom and some milestones in Latin America such as Mexico and Brazil. At each annual edition of this seminar, there is always an insightful student who asks what was happening with the curriculum in Argentina in the meantime.

Talking with William Pinar in one of the meetings offered by the internationalization of the curriculum, I told him about the way in which I had organized the seminar to teach Curriculum Theory to students who did not know the field. Pinar replied provocatively: "That's the history of the United States!" True, the official history of curriculum is the history of U.S. education. But what other history could be taught in Curriculum Theory to provoke the necessary break in studying postcritical curriculum theories in Latin America. Without delving into the plot of U.S. technicality, Latin American curriculum thinking could never be genuine. How can such a traumatic beginning be avoided if Latin America recognizes the curriculum from the 1950s, in the case of Brazil, and from the 1960s for the rest of the countries. If its entry into the field is through the pragmatism of the "Tyler Rationale", what other possibilities are there to begin the study of curriculum theory than by unveiling the myth of this beginning? Only a political imperative allows us to teach this subject by offering sufficient resistance to the hegemony that the United States exercised over the rest of the continent. The United States, which became the first American country to gain independence from the colony, to treat slavery, negritude and indigenism as problems derived from cultural dependence and colonization, marks the beginning of curriculum theory. Slavery, negritude, indigeneity, are American problems that stain the map from Canada to Argentina, from the Andes to the ocean, and yet, seem to be only US problems. More than the deployment of an identity, for Laclau and Mouffe (2010) hegemony is the response to a crisis to fill a vacuum.

There are always other ways of teaching, always. What is difficult is to reconstruct a biased history without protagonists or antecedents. Because the colonialism doubly suffered by the Latinos of America, we are burdened with the foreignness of the migrations that installed us in this territory and the hegemony of one of our own that keeps the history and the names to itself. There are other ways of teaching curriculum theory in Latin America other than demonstrating the technical and instrumental "beginning" of the curriculum and the contemporary silencing of Dewey when he presented a notion of curriculum influenced by the ideas of Herbart's pedagogy and *Bildung* ideal of formation, it only remains to materialize other pieces that power and emptiness still leave invisible.

Inspired by Lazzarato (2006) I ask what possibility this event leaves for Latin American subjects; that in the first half of the 20th century curriculum production was concentrated at the University of Chicago. I agree with Badiou (2013) when he argues that an event is rupture and possibility. And rather than denying of the history of the curriculum, what I find is the possibility of constructing the history and epistemology of the Latin American curriculum with another approach, with other subjects, recognizing other circumstances. Now, to the extent that we cannot find another way of teaching curriculum theory, this option continues to be the crisis that attempts to fill a vacuum, as Laclau and Mouffe make clear when they refer to hegemony.

The traces of curriculum history written up to then from Latin America, serve to occupy with "language game" as Wittgenstein (2021/1953) taught, the spaces that no one else but hegemony has occupied. With the event, the impossible becomes possible through collective work. I agree with the suspicion of the foundational moments and the rejection of the origin. But I accept the event in the history of societies as the rupture that removes the veil of conformity, the *status quo* and naturalization. It is in the rupture as an interstice (historical, social, cultural, subjective, theoretical) that the possibility of doing something different to teach the theory/s of the curricula in (Latin) America is lodged.

As if it were an interactive puzzle, all of America is assembled by colonizations, migrations, violence of all kinds that silence voices, erase cultures, neutralize languages, discriminate races, annihilate lives. It is necessary to place ourselves in the rupture as an intermediate space to question the hegemony with which the history of the curriculum is recognized, with its technical, rational and efficient perspective that guarantees social control and annuls the differences of practices. The neo-technicism of the 1990s is nothing more than the usufruct by the hegemony of technical rationality, but this time with the conviction that there was no other alternative and that the re-edition of the history of the curriculum once again fills a void. Guidelines that order and control was once again the constant that, under the logic of globalization, gives relevance to the curricular discourse. The curricular discourse occupies the center of hegemony, empowers those who write about it, and makes visible those who work in the name of the curriculum. As a subjective construction, the event takes on materiality if there is disturbance in the social subjects who wonder what is happening to *them*. What is happening to them that they are disturbed by what they were not disturbed by before. This is how internationalization is the metaphor of that disturbance that makes the academics of the curriculum look with strangeness at their own field, feeling disturbed in the recognition of efficiency and *accountability*. Metaphor of disruption that materializes with multiculturalism (Macedo, 2015) and complicated conversation (Pinar, 2012, 2014b) and is identified as the opportunity for Latin American curriculum studies. It confronts the globalizing event in order to break the technicist hegemony that, together with the snatching of the signifier to the continent, intended to snatch the stories of the curriculum.

Imported models and translation

Chapter 3 has already dealt with translation as an intellection of curriculum policies, where they are recognized as a political text by means of deconstruction. Without abandoning poststructuralism, I notice in translation one of the marks of the curriculum in its relationship with the hegemony of the United States, as an exporter of technical rationality. This is how *Basic Principles of Curriculum and Instruction* by Ralph Tyler, with its first edition in 1973 and the fourth in 1982; *Curriculum Development, Theory and Practice* by Hilda Taba, with its first edition in 1974 and its seventh edition in 1987; *Curriculum Planning for Modern Schools* by J. Galen Saylor and William Alexander in 1970; Taxonomy of Educational Objectives by Benjamin Bloom, Max Engelhart, Edward Furst, Walter Hill and David Kranthwohl, which was published as "Bloom and collaborators" in at least 8 editions were translated. Robert Gagne's books, *The Condition of Learning and the Theory of Instruction* translated in 1979 with at least four editions and *Principles of Instructional Design* in 1976; *Systematic Instruction* by James Popham and Eva Baker, published since 1970. The literature translated from the U.S. curriculum field focused on guidelines for instructional planning through the design of objectives and guidelines for assessment. As a characteristic of this paradigm, the Psychology of Learning is used to refer to the curriculum. Jerome Seymour Bruner's *The Process of Education*, which arrived in 1963, and then *Toward a Theory of Instruction* were also translated. It is symptomatic to note how in Latin America a selective synthesis of U.S. curricular instrumentalism was reproduced. The tripod formed by objectives, assessment and learning accounted for a curricular model that had been sentenced to oblivion by the United States after the launching of Sputnik and the medical report issued by Joseph Schwab in 1969.

Derrida (1975, 2017) states that translation is impossible, because it is never saturated, it has no final moment in which it is decided to be "complete". Deconstruction decomposes the meaning of the text which, aided by betrayal, deceives the reader. However, this philosophical task of translation that makes it an act of "the political" can become an act of "the political" when the end is governance and agency. Then the selection for translation, as happened with the educational tasks of Alliance for Progress, becomes a "selective translation". It means that it determines a single meaning of the text (in the best sense of Laclau's empty signifier), which is oriented toward reproduction. This is the way in which the United States offered Latin America the reproduction of an educational failure in the name of the curriculum. If America is colonized in 1492, "selective translation" can be recognized as another moment of colonization, albeit with the misfortune of being experienced internally. One of the children of the colony learned the languages of the conquest faster than the rest.

In Argentina in the 1990s, a few years after leaving the dictatorship, we found ourselves fighting against the privatization of education and the standardized evaluations proposed by the curricular discourses. We were engaged in an intellectual struggle through philosophy in a postponed study of the "Teoría de los intereses constitutivos" (Theory of Constitutive Interests) that Habermas had published in *Conocimiento e Interés* (Knowledge and Interest) in 1968 and the *Teoría de la Acción Comunicativa* (Theory of Communicative Action), that arrived to Argentina, through Spain, in 1987. The reading of Habermas revived the study of the Frankfurt School with the criticisms of technical rationality made by Theodor Adorno and Max Horkheimer. Professor José Sazbón, of the National University of La Plata, an expert on this subject, recommended to his doctoral thesis students the study of these texts in German, avoiding selective translations, through which the reader was deceived rather than betrayed by the text. Regarding Habermas and the Critical Theory of the Frankfurt School, this was also a reading chosen, in the same decade, by the Brazilian constellation (Pinar, 2011b, p. 15).

I recognize as another colonization the translation carried out by academics in Spanish universities from the mid-1980s onwards. After the end of the dictatorships in Latin America, there was a restructuring of teaching, which left behind the technicality to give way to the development of the school class, the particularity of the practice and the role of the teacher as the protagonist of the curriculum. José Gimeno Sacristán and Miguel Ángel Pérez Gómez made the first compilations of texts that, had it not been for them, would have taken longer to discover in the Latin American curriculum. In 1985 Gimeno Sacristán and Pérez Gómez published *La enseñanza, su teoría y su práctica* (Teaching, Theory and Practice). It consisted of a compilation of texts derived from the field of curriculum and the didactic tradition. For the section dedicated to Curriculum Theory, the compilers selected the following essays: "The Practical: A Language for Curriculum" by Joseph Schwab (1969); "The Moribund Curriculum Field: It's Wake and our Work" by Dwayne Huebner (1976); "Curriculum Theory: Gime Me a for Instance" by Herbert Kliebard (1977); "The Reconceptualization of Curriculum Studies" by William Pinar (1978); "Curriculum Studies: Reconceptualism or Reconstruction" by Martin Lawn and Lean Barton (1980). This section of the book allowed us to recognize the existence of something called "Curriculum Theory", which we quickly began to understand was more than one theory. However, that compilation sounded like a tight synthesis for those of us who were eager to study curriculum, since Schwab was presented only in his first essay on The Practical series. I admit that the following three essays were never translated into Spanish and that to get them I had to be logged in as a visitor at the Special Collections Research Center of the University of Chicago Library on the occasion of consulting "Joseph J. Schwab Papers". The relationship between the two moments in Schwab's academic life, the "first Schwab" who participates in the Biological Sciences Curriculum Study (BSCS) within the reform based on the structure of the disciplines (Morelli, 2011) with the "second Schwab" who theorizes about the field of curriculum, provoking the turn to practice, is also not explained. Another waste in translation were the works of Pinar, whose chapter written for *New directions in curriculum studies* edited by Philip Taylor was the only one that resonated under the reconceptualization movement in the field of curriculum in the United States. In this case, it remained unknown from the author his perspective regarding *currere*, gender, feminism, autobiography, and curriculum as a racial text. Only in 2014 José María García Garduño translates into a book entitled *La teoría del curriculum* (Curriculum Theory) a compilation of works focused on the movements of the field in the United States from 1950 with the crisis, reconceptualization and internationalization, gender and the study, among others. However, in that work, the betrayal of the text modifies the notion of curriculum as "complicated conversation" to curriculum as "complex conversation". I also highlight the loss of meaning when *Bildung* is translated as education and *Didaktik* as didactics, without further argumentation.

To close the chapter on technicism in Ibero-American societies, which share between them having been governed by dictatorships until the mid-1970s in the case of Spain and Portugal and until the mid-1980s in the American cases, Gimeno Sacristán made, in 1982, an illuminating critique of Tyler and Bloom in a book entitled *La pedagogía por objetivos. Obsesión por la eficiencia* (Pedagogy by Objectives: Obsession with Efficiency). I admit that the contribution of the Spanish translations was the opening to the practical and critical perspectives of the curriculum. Editorial Morata is one of the publishers that distributed the most translated works on curriculum. Thus, in 1988, it translated *Curriculum Theorising: Beyond Reproduction Theory* by Stephen Kemmis with the collaboration of Lindsay Fitzclarence (Kemmis and Fritzclarence, 1986); in 1991, *Curriculum: Product or Praxis*, by Shirley Grundy (1987); in 1992, *Between Education and Schooling: Outlines of a Diachronic Curriculum Theory* by Ulf Lundgren (1991) and in 1996, *Curriculum Evaluation in Schools* by Robert McCormick and Mary James (1983); in 1987, *An Introduction to Curriculum Research and Development* by Lawrence Stenhouse (1975) and in the same year, the selection of texts by Jean Rudduck and David Hopkins in 1985 entitled *Research as a Basis for Teaching* (1985). In 1994 Stephen Ball's compilation *Foucault and Education: Disciplines and Knowledge* (1991); in 1994 *The Structuring of Pedagogic Discourse* by Basil Bernstein (1990); in 1990 a compilation of texts on educational action research and curriculum by John Elliot; in 1994 *Evaluating with Validity* by Ernest House (1980); in 1991 *Life in Classrooms* by Philip Jackson (1968); in 1994 *A Political Sociology of Educational Reform* by Thomas Popkewitz (1991) and in 1994, *Race and Curriculum* by Cameron McCarthy (1990).

For many years I wondered whether I should have taken Professor Sazbón's advice and read the text in the original language. Although this would have disenchanted Derrida since it would have avoided the discursive conflict that triggers the translation, nullifying it completely. As a mark of conquest, the owner of the language shows again and again that the deception of the reader is not abandoned. The contradiction in deciding to translate curricular texts should be noticed by the academy of unsuspecting readers. I again acknowledge the relevance and the wisdom of the small sample offered by Gimeno Sacristán and Pérez Gómez on Schwab, Pinar, Huebner, etc. and on the sample chosen by Morata on Grundy, Lundgren, Ball and others. But I also recognize that, according to Prof. Sazbón's advice, reading without translation allows the construction of a particular intertextuality chosen by each reader, without betrayal or deception.

The alarming aspect of this conflict is the submission to the myth, as Derrida argues, where the reader prefers to adhere to the universality of the text, ignoring the betrayal that each translation entails. The alienated reading of the translated text ignores the subjectivity of the authors, the circumstances of their writing and the reasons why the text is deconstructed. The alienated reader in the myth ignores the plot of meanings of the text. It should be clarified that the myth places the readers in the centrality of language and makes them believe that they do not need to submit to any deconstruction. In my opinion, the readers in the field of the Latin American curriculum finds themselves in what Wang (2004) calls the "third place", creating an intermediate space between the hegemonic languages (English as the "lingua franca" and Spanish as the imposed language) and the translated text. In this intermediate space the readers feel the expropriation characteristic of a foreigner. And then they will have to disengage themselves from the intentionality of "the small sample" in order to elaborate their own text of the curricular studies.

All of America is a conquered continent that bears in its name the mark of that conquest. Our languages are imposed, as a result of the negation of other languages, the object of cultural subjugation. The academy cannot ignore the fact that these ways of naming, which seem familiar and feel like our own, are alien. Translation, as an impossible act, places the reader at the crossroads of having to choose between oblivion or negation. Forgetting that it is a small deconstructed sample, that it may have distorted meanings and that the meaning probably belongs to the translator rather than to the author. Or denial, avoiding the conflict of translation, preferring to annul any act of deconstruction. In this case, the naive reader denies the translation and ignores the linguistic filter of the culture that plays all the time with signifiers and meanings.

Resistance

The ambiguity of Latin America in curriculum studies makes it an arena that oscillates between the tradition of US technicism, with which it enters the world of curriculum, and the critical sociological proposals that understand education as a political act and the curriculum as its point of resistance. Dictatorships, revolutions, oppression, repression, exclusion, injustice, inequality allowed critical theory to flourish as a safeguard for curriculum studies. Paulo

Freire's emancipatory educational ideas lead to academics who, since 1980, have inscribed social praxis in the curriculum, turning it into a construction that acquires the forms and categories of politics. This is the identity of the curriculum in Latin America. With its hybridity, it crosses internal borders and solves the problems of poverty with scarcity. But it also resists the onslaught of hegemony with the imposition of models, languages and practices that do nothing more than highlight subalternity. The historical Latin American resistance is nothing more than a defense mechanism against the change of identity in a standardized globalization. It is enough to recognize every three years the results of the PISA tests and the inadequacy of Latin American curricular policies to avoid failure. Just as the educational system creates school failure as a category to identify socio-educational misfits, hegemony creates standardization to exclude sectors such as ours, which insistently occupy the last positions in the ranking. Or perhaps we should quote Galeano (2004, p. 363) when he states that "underdevelopment is not a stage of development. It is its consequence". So, resistance is the defense mechanism that allows the continent to maintain its identity. Without radicalized, particularized, and denaturalized analyses, which understand that differences are social, there will be no change to face the relevant portion of globalization, colonization (internal and external) or the policies of neoliberalism that do nothing but aggravate poverty and exclusion.

Latin American identity is also constructed in the tension between emancipation as a metaphor for the Cuban revolution and westernization as a metaphor for European and US progress. Latin America is always in an intermediate space between revolution and progress, belonging and exclusion, subjugation, and negation. In the intermediate places left by these interstices are the germs of the identity of the Latin American curriculum. It will have to abandon universality, question the myth and be suspicious of translation. As a territory born of hegemony in 1492, it oscillates between the Modernity that gave it structure and the postmodernity that warns it of the cracking of the idea of people, school and common curriculum; between the critical theory that provides it with categories for liberation and the postcritical theories that highlight minorities and their differences, allowing everything to be possible; between the globalization to which it was obligatorily invited to participate and the internationalization that allows it to hold complicated conversations with others that are just as different.

6 Final words

I wish I knew when something comes to an end. If so, I could have other attitudes, make other decisions, write differently. I doubt that this is the case of the field of curriculum in Latin America, which, due to the youth of its object, is just beginning to be written. For this field, there are still no final words, but simply some conclusions that close a state of reflection that may be retrieved again at any time by another scholar. I leave then in these paragraphs the unfinished progress of a complex object that has a short history, and that already presents its own constellations. I made visible, starting with the Alliance for Progress, which does not mean that it did not exist before, how the marks of the colony and the deception of the language of the conqueror stain notions of curriculum that imprint pragmatism for its elaboration and the control of practices. The colonizing event permeates the worst of translation practices. That, which shows that the text is betrayed to distort its meanings with intentions of domination. On the other hand, the inquisitorial sentence of the multilateral credit organizations on Latin American education confirms the subjugation controlled by the standardization that does not fit the measures of the continent. Nothing could be more inappropriate than reports and recommendations on the state of education based on foreign criteria and unattainable objectives. The scarce autonomy of Latin America to intervene, with authenticity, in its own educational system delimits the event-obligation to the fulfillment of reforms whose curricular structures were reproduced in an almost identical way in all the countries of Latin America. As if the curriculum took on the meaning of the race track, these countries were subjected to participate in it, knowing that they would start later, in unequal conditions and sentenced to occupy the last places at the finish line. The disadvantage that globalization offers Latin America shows with ample data that it is time to design other proposals that give another identity to the educational systems and improve the lives of its inhabitants. Badiou (2011b) argues that every event has its vanishing point and that of the Latin American curriculum is internationalization. This movement is simultaneously inward and outward. In the mid-1980s, the field of curriculum began to be discussed from critical and postcritical paradigms, with categories that on the one hand evidenced hegemony and

DOI: 10.4324/9781003475279-6

on the other elaborated their own text. I admit that the internationalization of curriculum studies in Latin America has its anteroom. A fertile ground in the critique of the Tyler Rationale creates the intellectual conditions for a critical reading of the field. In the mid-1980s Díaz Barriga (1988, 1994) manifests the technical dependence on the curriculum in the elaboration of programs and proposes another relationship with practice and subjects.

> The methodological proposal we make for the elaboration of programs is the product of reflection, analysis and questioning about the studies developed on curriculum theory described here, as well as reflection on our own practice in the elaboration of these programs, since we consider that the study of this practice is a fundamental source for conceptual elaboration, and constitutes an attempt to rethink educational problems based on categories that account for them, according to our reality.
>
> (Díaz Barriga, 1988, p. 31)

In addition, de Alba makes the first approaches to the study of the Latin American curriculum through articulations with Argentina in the research program "El curriculum universitario frente a los retos del siglo XXI. Perspectivas de Mexico and Argentina" (The University Curriculum Facing the Challenges of the 21st century. Perspectives from Mexico and Argentina) (de Alba, 1998). In this program, the author states in the introduction to the report:

> Finally, to conclude this introduction, it should be emphasized that the panoramic studies presented below constitute one of the starting points for approaching the object of study of our research: the expectations of academics in public universities (in Mexico and Argentina) regarding the challenges of the curriculum in the 21st century.
>
> (de Alba, 1998, p. 15)

Likewise, for the case of Brazil, Kumar (2011b) states that curriculum studies in Brazil have, between 1980 and the mid-1990s, undergone a critical-Marxist stage:

> Abraham Magendzo's *Curriculum e cultura na América Latina* [Curriculum and Culture in Latin America] was also an important reference for the first courses introduced in Brazil. Antonio Flavio Barbosa Moreira's *Currículos e programas no Brasil* [Curricula and Programs in Brazil] became a key indeed canonical text.
>
> During the first half of the 1990's articles on the New Sociology of Education, then a subject little known to Brazilians, began to circulate, introduce by Brazilian scholars who had obtained their doctoral degrees in the United Kingdom, among then Antônio Flávio and Lucíola Licínio dos Santos. Such critical scholarship focused on the selection and distribution

> of school knowledge, an attempt "to understand relationships between the processes of selection, distribution and organization and teaching of school content and the strategies of power inside the inclusive social context". In their *Currículo, cultura e sociedade*, Moreira and Silva defined curriculum as school content; they also identified ideology, power, and culture as the main themes of the curriculum theory.
>
> (Kumar, 2011b, p. 28)

Thus, I intend to prove that before the institutionalization of internationalization, the field in Latin America was already being analyzed by critiques that questioned the dependence on US pragmatism and the conceptual limitations of this model. Had it not been for critical studies, the dialogues proposed by internationalization would not have received as they were. The event-internationalization establishes the solidarity ties necessary for conversations between regions and relations outside the Latin American territory, where similar paths were being taken.

Internationalization allows intellectuals of the curriculum to take cuttings of this complex and unapproachable object, composing it in parts. This is how Díaz Barriga and García Garduño (2014) coordinate a proposal involving ten countries, the dialogues between Casimiro Lopes and de Alba (2014) and de Alba and Casimiro Lopes (2015) and the coordination of Morelli (2021) involving the curriculum policies of Argentina, Mexico and Brazil. I also consider as part of this series the spaces created by the Mexican academy, at IISUE-UNAM, since 1990 for the debate on the Latin American curriculum (Gallardo Gutiérrez, 2023). There are also proposals edited by non-Latinos such as those of Pinar (2003a, 2011b, 2011c, 2014a) that construct archaeologies of the field. As a complex object, it will probably never be fully addressed. Multiple cuttings remain to be studied. What about curriculum studies in the Caribbean, Cuba and Panama. The relationship between Latin America and Canada, Bolivia's resistance that brings curriculum studies closer to indigenous populations. What other constellations can the vastness of Brazil offer, whether or not derived from UERJ education. How to articulate the production of Colombia, what about the recent official arrival of Argentina in the field of curriculum. Will there ever be Mercosur curriculum studies? What contributions can the Uruguayan academy make? What about Afro-America? What about indigenous peoples? How is gender represented in Latin American curriculum studies in a region with sexist social, labor and cultural relations? The questions can go on in an attempt to demarcate an ambiguous and complex object, riddled with minimal experiences and hidden histories that have not yet been written. However, every time a Latin American tells an intellectual history or a present circumstance about the curriculum (Pinar, 2011b, 2011c), he or she will be doing so for the field of curriculum in (Latin) America.

The first task, in my opinion, is to define the relations with the United States and European countries as providers of theories and perspectives of analysis that have affected the field. The difficult task of questioning the theories with which we have been formed merits an exercise in deconstruction that uproots colonialism with Europe and the United States. Naturalized relations of subalternity that condition curriculum theory and school practices. Conquests, migrations and translations have time and again strengthened and confirmed dependency, deciding where to oppress. That is to say, what aspect of the curriculum to communicate, hide, distort, changing signifiers and reducing publications. This path, controlled by the hegemony of conquest, was also fertile ground for the disembarkation of multilateral credit organizations in the financing of curricular reforms in 1990. Adherence to models of curricular pragmatics guaranteeing educational quality and social welfare was as automatic as it was imposed, without the possibility of offering counter-arguments that would allow for other more autochthonous curricular constructions. Just like the lost race of PISA, a global evaluation elaborated with standards foreign to Latin American curricular development. It is not that Latin American curricula enjoy good health and proposals. On the contrary. But if the evaluation of unwise practices is carried out with foreign criteria, it makes no sense to evaluate.

The construction of post-*Bildung* for the process of formation of a post-pandemic Latin American subject call for solidarity as the third moment of the *didaktik* centered on *Bildung*, as presented by Klafki (1998). But also to attend to the metaphorical fiction of literature and its characters, who carry the problems of femininities, negritudes and disabilities, narrated in first person, in Latin American territories. In relation to art, recovering the literary genre known as *Bildungsroman*, it will be necessary to create characters who resist the circumstances of their formation processes, who reflect on their identity and what they want to become. But in addition, Post-*Bildung* will make sense if it incorporates the debate of the subject configured by multiple literacies in which the force of the Moving Image is greater than that of writing. The screen as a renewed *black mirror* returns the density of a distorted identity, filtered, modified by the aesthetics of consumption. It is more profitable to show happiness than intelligence, it is more profitable the capacity of consumption than the formation of the subject. In the year 2022 I accompanied residents of Educational Sciences of the UNR in the development of a workshop called *Odisea* (Odyssey). In it we proposed to 17 and 18 year-olds, who were finishing high school, reflections on identity and the future. Guided by the classic questions "who am I" and "what do I want to become", a pedagogical debate was provoked where the workshop participants could reflect on themselves. To our surprise, those who chose to participate in the workshop were all women. Their concerns revolved around hypocrisy, social simulation, lack of ethics with the environment, the privileges with which their parents raised their male siblings but not them, and the future of their own lives when they finish high school. Working with them allowed me to confirm the power of these two questions, with the solidity of a formation theory and a pedagogical framework for the process. But since the workshops took place in the school, it also served to confirm that the secondary school is in a position to deal with issues of formation that are more social and cultural than disciplinary. Although the idea of *Bildung* was part of Lyotard's (2004/1979) critique of the modern project, I do not find it incongruous that little stories and narrative knowledges are part of post-*Bildung*. Without wishing to be apocalyptic or to suggest that the concept of (post) *Bildung* will be the salvation of the subject through its formation, I consider it pertinent to attend to the pedagogical core, of relationship with others and of reflection with oneself that it proposes in order to rethink the subject of postmodernity. On the other hand, *Bildung* has the articulatory capacity to find a place between curriculum theory and *didaktik* tradition. As it happened with the character of Camila or the young women of the *Odisea* workshop, there are problems installed by the force of the culture and the history of the continent associated with the disadvantages toward women, due to their feminine condition alone. I turn to solidarity as the third moment referred to by Klafki (1998) to face the decisions of the silenced Latin American voices so that the process of formation makes the subject visible and vice versa.

It is essential not to neglect curriculum policies as an object of study for curriculum scholars. The first task remains that of distinguishing between what corresponds to the field of educational policies and what we identify in curriculum policies. Mouffe's (2014, p. 22) agonist theory provides the differentiation between the political and politics, defining the latter as "the set of practices, discourses and institutions that seeks to establish a certain order and organize human coexistence in conditions that are always potentially conflictive." In the recognition of an adversary, rather than an enemy, there will always be an *other* to converse about curriculum decisions, approaching Pinar's (2011a, 2012) complicated conversation. Derrida's (1975, 2017) translation theory allows us to understand that there will be changes in the curriculum text each time it moves from one level to another. To pretend that the universality of policies reaches the school intact is the pragmatic fallacy that has been maintained for decades in this part of the continent and from which we are still not completely free of. Accepting non-linearity for the translation of policies, their vanishing points as opportunities for the different and that school practice will always be under the orbit of the uncontrolled, is part of the poststructuralist contributions to curricular policies. Neither from the top down, nor from the bottom up, as I said in Chapter 3. The entry of politics into the curriculum will be through any of the levels. Whenever there is an interstice caused by the tension between the political and the policy, there will be the possibility of creating something different in the curriculum. I redeem Priestley and Xenophontos (2021) when they identify the capacity of the teacher as the maker of the curriculum, to which I have added the teacher as translator and author of the curriculum, in the school. This is the proposal offered by "La Nueva Escuela Mexicana" (The New Mexican School) when it refers to "co-design" as the act in which the teacher designs assuming the regionalization of contents according to the local and contextual character

(*Plan de Estudios para la Educación Básica 2022*, pp. 11–12). The curriculum needs to reach the school and the classroom in a political manner. For practices to make sense, for teachers to feel protagonists and for solidarity to be a pedagogical task.

> For those who conceive history as a competition, Latin America's backwardness and misery are nothing more than the result of its failure. We lost; others won. But it so happens that those who won did so thanks to the fact that we lost: the history of Latin America's underdevelopment integrates, as it has been said, the history of the development of world capitalism.
>
> (Galeano, 2004, p. 16)

There are still texts to be written, stories to be redeemed, colleagues to be met in the young and resilient field of the Latin American curriculum.

References

Adorno, T. (1969). La educación después de Auschwitz. *Sur*.

Angulo Villanueva, R., Moreno Martínez, N. and Pérez García, A. (2023). Los padres opinan sobre la formación. La voz del imaginario colectivo. *El cardo*, n°19.

Angulo Villanueva, R. (2022). Código Curricular Emergente: Las voces del imaginario social. *Revista Espaço do Currículo,* v. 15, n. 2, p. 1–16, 2022. DOI: https://doi.org/10.15687/rec.v15i2.63680.

Angulo-Villanueva, R. and Reducindo-Ruiz, I. (2023). El pensamiento joven como desafío para la interacción entre docente y alumno en el marco del currículum vivido y la Covid-19 en 2020. In Barrón Tirado, M. (Coodinadora), *Currículum, subjetividades y nuevas tecnologías.* IISUE Educación, pp. 159–207.

Appadurai, A. (2001). *La modernidad desbordada: dimensiones culturales de la globalización*. Fondo de Cultura Económica.

Apple, M. (1986). *Ideología y Curriculum*. Akal.

Apple, M. (1987). *Educación y Poder*. Paidós.

Apple, M (2002). *Educar "como Dios manda". Mercados, niveles, religión y desigualdad.* Paidós.

Asensi Pérez, M. (2012). Los orígenes de la deconstrucción. In J. Derrida (Ed.), *La escritura y la diferencia.* Siglo XXI Grupo Editorial, pp. I–XV.

Badiou, A. (2011a). Pensar el acontecimiento. In A. Badiou y S. Žižek (Eds.), *Filosofía y actualidad.* Amorrortu, pp. 13–46.

Badiou, A. (2011b) *Pequeño panteón ilustrado.* Fondo de cultura económica.

Badiou, A. (2013). *La filosofía y el acontecimiento*. Amorrortu.

Ball, S. (1991). *Foucault and Education: Disciplines and Knowledge*. Routledge.

Barrón Tirado, M. (2020). La educción en línea. Transmisiones y disrupciones. In *Educación y Pandemia. Una visión académica* (pp. 66–74). IISUE.

Barrón Tirado, M. (2023). (Coordinadora). *Currículum, subjetividades y nuevas tecnologías.* IISU Educación.

Barros, I. y Días, R. (2023). Entre a BNCC e o sentido de comum: pensando o liberalismo e a democracia. *Currículo sem Fronteiras, 23.* Article e1 1133

Belleza, E. (2023). A vida como projeto na escola. *Currículo sem Fronteiras, 23.* Article e1138. http://dx.doi.org/10.35786/1645-1384.v23.1138

Bernstein, B. (1990). *The Structuring of Pedagogic Discourse. Volume IV: Class, codes and control.* Routledge.

Biesta, G. (2002). How General Can *Bildung* Be? Reflections on the Future of a Modern Educational Ideal. *Journal of Philosophy of Education, 36*(3).

Braidotti, R. (2015). *Lo posthumano.* Gedisa.

Buenfil, R. (1995). Horizonte posmoderno y configuración social. In A. de Alba (comp.), *Posmodernidad y educación*. Porrúa, pp. 11–67.

Camilo Costa, H. (2021). Pensar as políticas de currículo: impressões no debate sobre raciocínio geográfico. *Revista Signos Geográficos*, 3, 1–20. https://revistas.ufg.br/signos/article/view/70139

Camilo Costa, H. and Casimiro Lopes, A. (2011). Integração, Inter|disciplinariedade e geografia em propostas curriculares nacionais. In L. Casimiro, D. Evangelista and R. Gomes de Abreu (Eds.), *Discursos nas políticas de currículo*. Quartet, pp. 77–118.

Casimiro Lopes, A. (2011). Libraries and Identities. In W. Pinar (Ed.), *Curriculum Studies in Brazil. Intellectual Histories, Present Circumstances*. Palgrave Macmillan, pp. 115–169.

Casimiro Lopes, A. (2013). Teorias pós-críticas, política e currículo. *Educação, Sociedade & Culturas*, (v.39), pp. 7–23.

Casimiro Lopes, A., Da Cucha, E. y Costa, H. (2013). Da recontextualização à tradução: investigando políticas de currículo. *Currículo sem Fronteiras, 13*(3), pp. 392–410.

Casimiro Lopes, A., Evangelista Dias, R. and Gomes de Abreu, R. (2011). *Discursos nas políticas de currículo*. Quartet.

Casimiro Lopes, A. and Macedo, E. (2011). *Teorias de currículo*. Cortez Editora.

Casimiro Lopes, A. and de Alba, A. (2014). (Organização). *Diálogos curriuclares entre Brasil e México*. Ed. UERJ.

Casimiro Lopes, A. and Macedo, E. (2014). Movimientos recientes en el campo del curriculum en Brasil: articulaciones entre perspectivas posestructuralistas y marxistas. In A. Díaz-Barriga y J. García Garduño (Eds.), *Desarrollo del curriculum en América Latina. Experiencia en diez países*. Miño y Dávila Editores, pp. 89–104.

Chehaibar Nader, L. (2020). Flexibilidad curricular. Tensiones en tiempos de pandemia. In: Barrón Tirado, M. (Coordinadora). *Educación y Pandemia. Una visión académica*, pp. 66–74, IISUE Educación.

Coll Salvador, C., Díaz Barriga Arcedo, F., Engel Rocamora, A. y Salina Ibáñez, J. (2023). Evidencias de aprendizaje en prácticas educativas mediadas por tecnologías digitales. *RIED-Revista Iberoamericana de Educación a Distancia, 26*(2), pp. 9–25.

de Alba, A. (1995). *Curriculum: crisis, mito y perspectiva*. Miño y Dávila Editores.

De Alba, A. (1998). Introducción al desarrollo del campo del curriculum universitario en las últimas dos décadas: los casos de México y Argentina. In: De Alba, A., Chehaibar, L. Dosba de Duluc, S. Marengo, R. y Puiggrós, A. (1995). *Panorama del currículum universitario 1970–1990: México y Argentina*. Cuadernos del CESU 33, pp. 9–16.

de Alba, A. (2007). *Curriculum-sociedad. El peso de la incertidumbre, la fuerza de la imaginación*. IISUE Educación, Plaza y Valdés Editores.

De Alba, A. and Casimiro Lopes, A. (2015) (Coordinadoras). *Diálogos curriculares entre México y Brasil*. IISUE Educación.

de Alba, A. (2021). La construcción de la presencialidad en la virtualidad como exigencia político-pedagógica. *Revista Argentina de Investigación Educativa, I*(1), pp. 13–29.

Derrida, J. (1997). La farmacia de Platón. In: Derrida, J. *La diseminación*. Espiral-ensayos, pp. 91–261.

Derrida, J. (2012). *De la gramatología*. Siglo XXI Editores.

Derrida, J. (2017). Carta a un amigo japonés. In: Derrida, J. *El tiempo de una tesis. Descontrucción e implicaciones conceptuales*. Anthropos, pp. 23–27.

Díaz Barriga, A. (1988). *Didáctica y curriculum*. Nuevomar.

Díaz Barriga, A. (1994). *Docente y programa. Lo institucional y lo didáctico.* Aique Grupo Editor.

Díaz Barriga, A. (2011). Curriculum Studies in Mexico: Origin, Evolution, and Current Circumstances. In W. Pinar (Ed.), *Curriculum Studies in Mexico. Intellectual Histories, Present Circumstances.* Palgrave Macmillan , pp. 91–109.

Díaz Barriga, A. y García Garduño, J. (Coordinadores). (2014). *Desarrollo del curriculum en América Latina. Experiencia en diez países.* Miño y Dávila Editores.

Díaz Barriga-Arceo, F. and Barrón Tirado, M. (2020). Currículo y pandemia: Tiempo de crisis y oportunidad de innovación disrupción. *Revista Electrónica Educare, 24*(Suplemento especial), pp. 7–11.

Díaz Barriga Arceo, F. & Barrón Tirado, M. (2022). Desafíos del currículo en tiempo de pandemia: innovación disruptiva y tecnologías para la inclusión y justicia social. *Revista electrónica de investigación educativa,* 24, e10. https://doi.org/10.24320/redie.2022.24.e10.4500

Díaz Barriga-Arceo, F. and Barrón Tirado, M. (2023). El currículo en la educación superior mexicana en el contexto de la pospandemia. *El cardo,* n°19.

Díaz Barriga-Arceo, F., Alatorre-Rico, J. and Castañeda-Solís, F. (2022). Trayectorias interrumpidas: motivos de estudiantes universitarios para suspender temporalmente sus estudios durante la pandemia. *Revista Iberoamericana de Educación Superior* (ries), *XIII*(36), pp. 3–25.

Dickens, C. (2014). *David Copperfield.* Alianza Editorial.

Evangelista Dias, R. (2011). Demandas sobre integração nas políticas curriculares da formação de professores. In L. Casimiro, R. Evangelista Dias and R. Gomes de Abreu (Eds.), *Discursos nas políticas de currículo.* Quartet , pp. 225–244.

Evangelista Dias, R. and Bastos Craveiro, C. (2011). Políticas curriculares nacionais para a formação da identidade docente. In: Casimiro Lopes, Evangelista Dias, R. and Gomes de Abreu, R. (2011). *Discursos nas políticas de currículo.* Quartet, pp. 185–204.

Evangelista Dias, R. (2019). A docência como fator de qualidade para educação. In E. Macedo and I. Menezes (Org.), *Currículo, política e cultura. Conversas entre Brasil e Portugal.* CRV Editora, pp. 75–93.

Evangelista Dias, R. Borges, V. and de Oliveira, M. (2023). *Docência nas políticas de currículo na Ibero-América. Demandas em disputa.* CVR.

Fabre, M. (2011). Experiencia y formación: la Bildung. *Revista Educación y Pedagogía, 23*(59), enero–abril, pp. 215–225.

Frangella, R. (2018). Do silêncio e seus sons: "diferenças" na Base Nacional Comun Curricular. In: Casimiro Lopes, A., Martins de Oliviera, A. and Sousa de Oliveira, G. (Org.) *Os gêneros da escola. E o (im)possível silenciamento da diferença no currículo.* Editora UFPE, pp. 163–186.

Freud, S. (1981/1911). Los dos principios del funcionamiento mental. In *Obras completas.* Tomo 2. Biblioteca Nueva, pp. 1638–1642.

Galeano, E. (2004). *Las venas abiertas de América Latina.* Catálogos.

Gallardo Gutiérrez, A. (2015). Justicia curricular y curriculum intercultural. Notas conceptuales. In A. de Alba y A. Casimiro Lopes (Eds.), *Diálogos curriculares entre México y Brasil.* IISUE Educación, pp. 65–79.

Gallardo Gutiérrez, A. (2017). The Culture and the Mexican Basic Education. *Transnational Curriculum Inquiry,* Special Issue: Voices, Tensions and Perspectives of Curriculum, *14*(1–2), pp. 83–86.

Gallardo Gutiérrez, A. (2021). Conflictos epistemológicos en torno a las políticas curriculares de la educación básica mexicana. In S. Morelli (Coord.), *Políticas curriculares. Experiencias en contextos latinoamericanos.* Homo Sapiens Ediciones, pp. 177–196.

Gallardo Gutiérrez, A. (2023). Tácticas intersticiales y nuevas formas de subjetivación digital. Apuntes en torno a un modelo didáctico del Seminario Currículum Latinoamericano. In M. Barrón-Tirado (Coodinadora), *Currículum, subjetividades y nuevas tecnologías.* IISU Educación, pp. 131–157.

García Canclini, N. (2007). *Culturas híbridas. Estrategias para entrar y salir de la modernidad.* Paidos.

García Garduño, J. (2011). Acculturation, Hybridity, Cosmopolitanism in Ibero-American Curriculum Studies. In W. Pinar (Ed.), *Curriculum Studies in Mexico. Intellectual Histories, Present Circumstances.* Palgrave Macmillan, pp. 137–163.

García Garduño, J. (2014). Estudio introductorio. In W. Pinar (Ed.), *La teoría del curriculum. Narcea*, pp. 11–59.

Gimeno Sacristán, J. y Pérez Gómez, A. (1985). *La enseñanza: su teoría y su práctica.* Akal.

Giroux, H. (1988). *Los profesores como intelectuales.* Paidos.

Granovsky, S. (2014). *El genocidio silenciado. Holocausto del pueblo armenio.* Ediciones Continente.

Hesse, H. (2018). *Demian.* Ediciones americanas.

Horlacher, R. (2016). *The Educated Subject and the German Concept of Bildung a Comparative Cultural History.* Routledge.

Horlacher, R. and De Vicenti, A. (2014). From Rationalist Autonomy to Scientific Empirism: A History of Curriculum in Switzerland. In W. Pinar (Ed.), *Internacional Handbook of Curriculum Research*, 2nd ed. Routledge, pp. 476–492.

House, E. (1980). *Evaluating and Validity.* Sage Publications Inc.

Huebner, D. (1976).The Moribund Curriculum Field: It's Wake and Our Work. *Curriculum Inquiry,* 6, pp. 153–167.

Jackson, P. (1991/1968). *La vida en las aulas.* Morata.

Kemmis, S. and Fritzclarence, L. (1986). *Curriculum Theorising: Beyond Reproduction Theory.* Deakin University.

Klafki, W. (1998). Characteristics of Critical Constructive Didaktik. In B. Gundem and S. Hopmann (Eds.), *Didaktik and/or Curriculum. An International Dialogue.* Peter Lang, pp. 307–330.

Kliebard, H. (1978). Curriculum theory: Give me a "for instance". *Curriculum Inquiry,* 6, pp. 257–269.

Klafki, W. (2015). The Significance of Classical Theries of Bildung for a Contemporary Concept of Allgemeinbildung. In: Westbury, I., Hopmann, S. and Riquartz, K. (eds.). *Teaching as a Reflective Practice. The German Didaktik Tradition.* Routledge, pp. 85–107.

Kumar, A. (2011a). Curriculum Studies in Mexico: An Overview. In W. Pinar (Ed.), *Curriculum Studies in Mexico. Intellectual Histories, Present Circumstances.* Palgrave Macmillan, pp. 29–48.

Kumar, A. (2011b). Curriculum Stuides in Brazil: An Overview. In W. Pinar (Ed.), *Curriculum Studies in Brazil. Intellectual Histories, Present Circumstances.* Palgrave Macmillan, pp. 27–42.

Laclau, E. (1993). *Nuevas reflexiones sobre la revolución de nuestro tiempo.* Nueva Visión.

Laclau, E. (1996). *Emancipación y diferencia*. Ariel.

Laclau, E. (2005). Desconstrucción, pragmatismo y hegemonía. In: Mouffe, C. (comp.) *Desconstrucción y pragmatismo*. Paidós, pp. 97–136.

Laclau, E. (2008). *La razón populista*. Fondo de Cultura Económica.

Laclau, E. y Mouffe, C. (2010). Hegemonía y estrategia socialista. Fondo de Cultura Económica.

Lawn, M. and Barton, L. (1980). Curriculum Studies: Reconceptualism or Reconstruction? *Journal of Curriculum Theorizing*. 2, pp. 47–56.

Lawrence, A. R. (2016). Review of *A Japanese Constellation: Toyo Ito, SANAA, and Beyond*. *Journal of the Society of Architectural Historians*, *75*(4), pp. 509–511. https://www.jstor.org/stable/26418954

Lazzarato, M. (2006). *Políticas del acontecimiento*. Tinta Limón.

Løvlie, L. (2002). The Promise of Bildung. *Journal of Philosophy of Education*, *36*(3), pp. 467–486.

Lundgren, U. (1991). *Teoría del curriculum y escolarización*. Morata.

Lyotard, J.-F. (2004/1979). *La condición posmoderna*. Cátedra.

Macedo, E. (2015). Curriculum, cultura y diferencia. In A. de Alba y A. Casimiro Lopes (Eds.), *Diálogos curriculares entre México y Brasil*. IISUE Educación, pp. 81–98.

Macedo, E. (2018). A teoria do currículo e o futuro monstro. In A. Casimiro Lopes y M. Siscar (Orgs.), *Pensando a política com Derrida*. Cortez Editora, pp. 153–177.

Macedo, E. (2021). Filantropía, iglesia y las recientes políticas curriculares en Brasil. In S. Morelli (Coord.), *Políticas curriculares. Experiencias en contextos latinoamericanos*. Homo Sapiens Ediciones, pp. 131–154.

Macedo, E. and Miller, J. (2022). Por um currículo "outro": autonomia e relacionalidade. *Currículo sem Fronteiras*, *22*, pp. 1–17.

Macedo, E. and Tomé, C. (2018). *Currículo e Diferença. Afectações em Movimento*. CRV Editora.

Martínez Delgado, M. (2015). La tensión particularidad-universalidad de la cultura. Reflexiones sobre escritura autobiográfica y formación de profesores. In A. de Alba y A. Casimiro Lopes (Eds.), *Diálogos curriculares entre México y Brasil*. IISUE Educación, pp. 101–118.

Mc Carthy, C. (1990). *Race and Curriculum*. Falmer Press.

McCormick, R. and James, M. (1983). *Curriculum Evaluation in Schools*. Croom Helm Ltd.

McLarnon, M., et al. (2016). The School Bus Symposium: A Poetic Journey of Co-created Conference Space. *Art/Research International: A Transdisciplinary Journal*, *1*(1), pp. 141–173.

Morelli, S. (2010). *El curriculum universitario. Entre la política y la academia, las demandas y las reformas*. Laborde Editor.

Morelli, S. (2011). Curriculum, alfabetización científica y cambio tecnológico. En R. Biolatto (comp.), *La enseñanza de las Ciencias*. Laborde Editor, pp. 77–89.

Morelli, S. (2016). *Las tensiones del curriculum. Debates político-educativos entre México y Argentina*. Miño y Dávila editores.

Morelli, S. (2021a). El porvenir de las políticas curriculares. In S. Morelli (Coord.), *Políticas curriculares. Experiencias en contextos latinoamericanos*. Homo Sapiens Ediciones, pp. 11–23.

Morelli, S. (2021b). Event, currere and the ignorant schoolmaster. *Prospects*, *50*, pp. 149–160.

Morelli, S. (2021c). Curriculum–Didaktik and Bildung: A Language for Teaching? In B. Green, R. Philip and M. Brennan (Eds.), *Curriculum Challenges and Opportunities in a Changing World. Transnational Perspectives in Curriculum Inquiry.* Palgrave McMillan, pp. 159–172.

Morin, E. (2001). *Introducción al pensamiento complejo*. Gedisa.

Mouffe, C. (2005). Desconstrucción, pragmatismo y la política de la democracia. In: Mouffe, C. (Comp.) *Desconstrucción y pragmatismo*. Paidós, pp. 13–33.

Mouffe, C. (2009). *En torno a lo político*. Fondo de Cultura Económica.

Mouffe, C. (2012). *La paradoja democrática. El peligro del consenso en la política contemporánea.* Gedisa.

Mouffe, C. (2014). *Agonística. Pensar el mundo políticamente*. Fondo de Cultura Economica.

Oliveira, D. and Frangella, R. (2022). Presentación del dossier: Currículos culturales extraescolares: sobre un campo en constante expansión, invención y creación para afirmar la vida. *Série Estudos - Revista del Programa de Postgrado en Educación de la UCDB*, *27*(61), pp. 3–12.

Orozco Fuentes, B. (2015). Apuntes para la reactivación del discurso teórico curricular en México. In A. de Alba y A. Casimiro Lopes (Eds.), *Diálogos curriculares entre México y Brasil.* IISUE Educación, pp. 25–41.

Orozco Fuentes, B. (2020). Interrogar el sentido del conocimiento escolar ante la pandemia. *Perfiles Educativos*, *XLII*(170), pp. 69–94.

Pérez Arenas, D. (2021). Currículum y docencia en tiempos de pandemia, desde una mirada epistémica-ontológica. *Kinesis. Revista Veracruzana de Investigación Docente*. Año, *6*(6), pp. 112–132.

Pinar, W. (1978): The Reconceptualisation of Curriculum Studies, *Journal of Curriculum Studies*, 10:3, pp. 205–214.

Pinar, W. (2003a). *International Handbook of Curriculum Research*. Lawrence Erlbaum Associates, Inc.

Pinar, W. (2003b). The Internationalization of Curriculum Studies. Keynote presented in XII Conference of the Mexican Council for Educative Investigation (COMIE) in Guadalajara, November 2003.

Pinar, W. (2006). *The Synoptic Text Today*. Peter Lang.

Pinar, W. (2011a). *The Character of Curriculum Studies*. Palgrave Macmillan.

Pinar, W. (2011b). (Ed.). *Curriculum Studies in Brazil. Intellectual Histories, Present Circumstances*. Palgrave Macmillan.

Pinar, W. (2011c). (Ed.). *Curriculum Studies in Mexico. Intellectual Histories, Present Circumstances*. Palgrave Macmillan.

Pinar, W. (2012). What Is Curriculum Theory? Routledge.

Pinar, W. (2013). *Curriculum Studies in the United States. Present Circumstances, Intellectual Histories*. Palgrave MacMillan.

Pinar, W. (2014a). (Ed.). *Internacional Handbook of Curriculum Research*, 2nd ed. Routledge.

Pinar, W. (2014b). *La teoría del curriculum*. Narcea.

Pinar, W., Reynolds, W., Slattery, P. and Taubman, P. (2008). *Understanding Curriculum*. Peter Lang.

Popkewitz, T. (1991). *A Political Sociology of Educational Reform. Power/Knowledge in Teaching, Teacher Education, and Research.* Teachers College, Columbia University.

Popkewitz, T. (1994). *Sociología política de las reformas educativas*. Morata.

Priestley, M. and Xenofontos, C. (2021). Curriculum Making Key Concepts and Practices. In J. Biddulph and J. Flutter (Eds.), *Inspiring Primary Curriculum Design*. Routledge, pp. 1–13.

Ramalho Ortigão, M. and Vidal Pereira, T. (2019). Trabalho colaborativo: conflito e dialogicidade. In E. Macedo and I. Menezes (Org.), *Currículo, política e cultura. Conversas entre Brasil e Portugal.* CRV Editora, pp. 95–109.

Ramos, A. and Frangella, R. (2014). Currículo, cultura e formação: desafios para a universidade frente às directrizes nacionais para a educação em direitos humanos. In A. Casimiro Lopes and A. de Alba (Org.), *Diálogos curriculares entre Brasil e México.* UERJ, pp. 229–255.

Ranniery, T. and. Macedo, E. (2018). Políticas do vivível: diferença, teoria e democracia por vir. In A. Casimiro Lopes, A. Martins de Oliviera and G. Sousa de Oliveira (Org.), Os gêneros da escola. *E o (im)possível silenciamento da diferença no currículo.* Editora UFPE, pp. 21–50.

Rudduck, J. and Hopkins, D. (1985). *Research as a Basis for Teaching*. Heinemann Educational Books Ltd.

Saied Méndez, Y. (2023). *Furia*. Vintage Español.

Salinger, J. (2014). *The Catcher in the Rye*. Litle, Brown and Company.

Schmelkes, S. (2009). *Características clave y retos del sistema educativo mexicano*. Universidad Iberoamericana. http://www.oecd.org/dataoecd/31/48/43758544.pdf

Schwab, J. (1969). The Practical: A Language for Curriculum. *The School Review*, *78*(1), pp. 1–23.

Scofano Medeiros, R. and Ranniery, T. (2018). Geografias da criação: currículo, espaço e diferença. In E. Macedo and C. Tomé (Eds.), *Currículo e Diferença. Afectações em Movimento*. CRV Editora , pp. 93–114.

Silva, T. (1997). El proyecto educacional moderno: ¿Identidad terminal? In: Veiga-Neto, A. *Crítica pos-estructuralista y educación*. Laertes, pp. 273–290.

Silva, T. (1999). *Documentos de identidade. Uma introdução às teorias do currículo*. Autentica.

Stable URL: https://www.jstor.org/stable/1084049

Stenhouse, L. (1975). *An Introduction to Curriculum Research and Development*. Heinemann Educational Books Ltd.

Verón, E. (1985). El análisis del "Contrato de Lectura", un nuevo método para los estudios de posicionamiento de los soportes de los media. *Les Medias: Experiences, recherches actuelles*, apl*ications* IREP.

Vidal Pereira, T. (2021). *Avaluação pedagógica. Limites e possibilidades*. CVR Editora.

Wang, H. (2004). *The Call from the Stranger on a Journey Home: Curriculum in a Third Space*. Peter Lang.

Westbury, I., Hopmann, S. and Riquartz, K. (2015). (Eds.). *Teaching as a Reflective Practice. The German Didaktik Tradition.* Routledge.

Wittgenstein, L. (2021/1953). *Investigaciones filosóficas*. Editorial Trota.

Young, M. (1981). *Knowledge and Control*. McMillan.

Young, M. (1989). Currículo e democracia: lições de uma crítica à nova sociologia da educação. *Educação e realidade*, Porto Alegre, *14*(1), pp. 29–40.

Young, M. (2000). *O currículo do futuro: da "Nova Sociologia da Educação" a uma teoria crítica do aprendizado*. Papirus.

Index

Note: Page numbers followed by "n" denote endnotes

For Product Safety Concerns and Information please contact our EU representative GPSR@taylorandfrancis.com
Taylor & Francis Verlag GmbH, Kaufingerstraße 24, 80331 München, Germany

www.ingramcontent.com/pod-product-compliance
Lightning Source LLC
LaVergne TN
LVHW010938110826
845149LV00013B/2657

* 9 7 8 1 0 3 2 7 5 7 0 3 2 *